"*Future Ready* is a step-by-step guide through the perilous journey of digital transformation. A must read for any business leader either embarking on or already engaged in the transformation challenge."

—**MAILE CARNEGIE,** Group Executive, Australian Retail, ANZ Bank

"*Future Ready* is a work of art—and usefulness. It moves from theory to practice and implementation, illustrating best practices by leading firms that have aligned their digital strategy and culture for success. Whether you are in the midst of your digital transformation or preparing for one, this book is required reading for your next phase."

—**BERNARD GAVGANI,** Group CIO, BNP Paribas

"*Future Ready* is an insightful and practical guide for competing in today's digital economy, where instant fulfillment, rapid innovation cycles, nontraditional competitors, and blurred industry boundaries are the new normal. The pathways and capability transformations set out in *Future Ready* will be helpful for senior managers everywhere."

—**JONATHAN LARSEN,** Chief Innovation Officer, Ping An Group; Chairman and CEO, Ping An Global Voyager Fund

FUTURE READY

FUTURE READY

THE FOUR PATHWAYS TO CAPTURING DIGITAL VALUE

STEPHANIE L. WOERNER
PETER WEILL
INA M. SEBASTIAN

Harvard Business Review Press
Boston, Massachusetts

Copyright 2022 Stephanie L. Woerner, Peter Weill, Ina M. Sebastian
Figures and tables copyright 2022 Massachusetts Institute of Technology

All rights reserved
Printed in the United States of America
10 9 8 7 6 5 4 3 2 1

No part of this publication may be reproduced, stored in or introduced into a retrieval system, or transmitted, in any form, or by any means (electronic, mechanical, photocopying, recording, or otherwise), without the prior permission of the publisher. Requests for permission should be directed to permissions@harvardbusiness.org, or mailed to Permissions, Harvard Business School Publishing, 60 Harvard Way, Boston, Massachusetts 02163.

The web addresses referenced in this book were live and correct at the time of the book's publication but may be subject to change.

Library of Congress Cataloging-in-Publication Data

Names: Woerner, Stephanie L., author. | Weill, Peter, author. | Sebastian, Ina M., author.
Title: Future ready : the four pathways to capturing digital value / Stephanie L. Woerner, Peter Weill, Ina M. Sebastian.
Description: Boston, Massachusetts : Harvard Business Review Press, [2022] | Includes index.
Identifiers: LCCN 2022013318 (print) | LCCN 2022013319 (ebook) | ISBN 9781647823498 (hardcover) | ISBN 9781647823504 (epub)
Subjects: LCSH: Organizational change. | Success in business. | Information technology—Management. | Business enterprises—Technological innovations.
Classification: LCC HD58.8 .W65 2022 (print) | LCC HD58.8 (ebook) | DDC 658.4/06—dc23/eng/20220625
LC record available at https://lccn.loc.gov/2022013318
LC ebook record available at https://lccn.loc.gov/2022013319

ISBN: 978-1-64782-349-8
eISBN: 978-1-64782-350-4

The paper used in this publication meets the requirements of the American National Standard for Permanence of Paper for Publications and Documents in Libraries and Archives Z39.48-1992.

Contents

Contents

FUTURE
READY

Chapter 1

Creating the Future-Ready Firm

As the world rapidly digitizes, firms are racing to first create new value from digital and then capture that value from digital in their financial performance.[1] A digital economy not only creates opportunities for many firms but also erects barriers to those firms that can't adapt fast enough. Think of Schneider Electric helping their customers reduce energy costs by up to 30 percent while generating half their revenue from IoT (Internet of Things) enabled services—developing this opportunity took vision, time, and investment that will be difficult to match. Or think of CEMEX creating an entirely new and much better way of inter-acting with jobsite managers with a mobile solution that simplifies ordering and payment and includes real-time tracking of delivery. Digitization makes real-time partnering easier. Think of WeChat in China, meeting the daily needs of customers with multiple partners offering complementary products. Or the US firm Fidelity Investments partnering with tax preparers, financial advice firms, and identity service providers to offer curated complementary services to their customers beyond Fidelity's core products.[2] Digitization also allows business processes to be made more modular, creating opportunities for faster innovation via reuse. Think of Amazon broadening their range of products from books to shopping to entertainment and, more recently, adding financial services components like loans and selling their underlying technology as a service via AWS (Amazon Web Services). We see the worth of firms like Amazon, Microsoft, and Facebook that leverage their platforms reflected in the stock market. More recently, we also see top-performing firms outside of the technology sector with digitally savvy leadership teams using the same approaches—like Charles Schwab, Visa, DBS, and Dunkin' Brands.[3] The goal is to develop the digital capabilities that enable a traditional firm to be a top performer in the digital economy—becoming a future-ready firm. This book is designed to be a playbook for firms to succeed in the digital economy, illustrated with motivating examples and data analyses that show how top performers operate differently. We include self-assessments to help leaders benchmark against top performers helping executives assess the opportunity and the progress of their transformation to becoming future ready.

What Is at Stake?

For many traditional firms, the viability of the existing business model is at stake. This point was hammered home to us in a workshop for a large bank—let's call them BankCo. This bank had operated successfully for more than one hundred years, making the majority of its profits through mortgages. It was once the go-to bank for mortgages in their major markets. But over time, intermediaries came between the bank and its customers.

The intermediaries came in many forms. The most common were mortgage brokers who offered their customers a choice of mortgage providers. These mortgage brokers were often traditional face-to-face businesses, but some were online businesses like Rocket Mortgage in the United States, Domain in Australia, and Habito in the United Kingdom. Over time, the percentage of mortgages originated through brokers grew to exceed 50 percent of the bank's mortgage book. Even more challenging was that the mortgage broker typically absorbed about 50 percent of the profit of the mortgage in upfront fees and sometimes trailing commissions and other payments. And most confounding was the difficulty to cross-sell other products even if the bank got the mortgage business since the mortgage broker had an existing relationship with the customer.

BankCo faced a serious business model choice and identified three options. Should they move toward the customer, offering a world-class mortgage experience and competing with their partners like the mortgage brokers? Or should they move away from the customer and become a world-class provider of "mortgages as a service" that is compliant with each country's regulatory environment? This option meant they were effectively selling an easy relationship with a combination of regulation/compliance and an attractive mortgage rate to any intermediary with an end customer that wanted a mortgage. They would be the PayPal of mortgages—instead of offering plug-and-play payment, they would provide a branded mortgage product that could seamlessly integrate into any other firm's platform. The third option was to do both. The problem with the third option was that the capabilities and organization needed to move toward the customer were very different from those needed for providing world-class mortgages to intermediaries.

Going toward the customer requires the ability to really listen and respond to the customer's voice and provide an amazing experience throughout the home purchasing journey. In contrast, moving away from the customer requires the creation of a world-class mortgage platform that can plug and play into any partner's systems. We will come back to BankCo in future chapters and share what happened next. Does your firm face this kind of transformation choice? Probably.

A Playbook to Capture Value from Digital

Transforming a firm to succeed in the digital economy requires a vision and a playbook to help firm leaders deliver on that vision, motivate employees, communicate with markets, and keep everyone focused on a common goal as they work to create new value in an increasingly digital world. The framework that we have developed starts with describing what it means to become a future-ready firm.

We define a firm undergoing a digitally enabled business transformation as having two simultaneous goals: (1) using digital technologies and practices to speed up and (2) wring out costs by standardizing and automating processes; reusing data, processes, and technology; and identifying areas where productivity can be increased. At the same time, these firms are using digital technologies and practices to innovate, creating new offers and services, identifying new ways to engage customers, and developing new business models and revenue streams. Some of the digital technologies and practices will provide efficiency gains and opportunities for innovation—for instance, service enabling a core capability with application programming interfaces (APIs)[4] standardizes and automates that capability, which can then be reused AND can potentially be bundled into a new product offering for customers.

We name firms that have learned to both improve customer experience and be more efficient, simultaneously and consistently, as future ready. Future-ready firms consider and use digital tools and approaches early in their decision-making to help address any challenge or opportunity, large or small. These digital tools and approaches include building and reusing platforms, test-and-learn techniques, agile methods, partnering to grow through digital connections, dashboards to accumulate and measure value, and many others. These future-ready firms are top performers, reporting estimated average revenue growth of 17.3 percentage points and a net margin of 14.0 percentage points above their industry average[5]—a rewarding premium.

We developed this playbook based on more than five years of rigorous research, including more than fifty interviews with executives and several surveys with a total of over two thousand respondents, and field-tested in multiple workshops with senior management teams and boards in firms across the world in diverse industries, plus many presentations and masterclasses.

Figure 1-1 describes the journey we recommend for leaders as they position their firms to become future ready and top performers in the digital economy.

- **Motivate:** Articulate your firm's purpose to your employees, managers, directors, and partners, and align it with the transformation to future ready. Digital business

1-1 Your Journey to Future Ready

Future Ready

Accumulate
value

Build
capabilities

Anticipate
the explosions

Commit
to a pathway

Motivate
with a strong purpose

transformation is challenging for the entire firm, and a strong purpose provides meaning to everyone on the journey.

- **Commit:** Choose one of the four pathways we have identified below, or progress on multiple pathways if your strategy dictates it. Communicate the pathway(s) and create a common language that everyone in the firm understands and uses to describe the journey.

- **Anticipate:** Look ahead to the common challenges—we call them organizational explosions—that occur in all digital business transformations and manage them.

- **Build:** Develop the ten capabilities future-ready firms have in common that help create value.

- **Accumulate:** Create, capture, and track three types of value—from operations, customers, and ecosystems—over time.

Setting the Context: The Future-Ready Firm

The two dimensions that firms improve on—operational efficiency and customer experience—create a 2×2 framework that describes four types of firms, with future-ready firms in the top right quadrant (see figure 1-2). Using multiple metrics for each dimension, we placed 1,311 firms on the future-ready framework relative to their competitors. The average estimated annual revenue of these firms was $4.8 billion.[6]

Silos and Spaghetti

Most large firms, typically with an extensive catalog of products developed or acquired over many years, start in the bottom left quadrant with traditional customer experience and operations. That's where 51 percent of firms sit—and the larger and older the firm, the more likely they are to be in this quadrant. They have a number of *silos* (sets of systems in a subset of a firm that support a business unit, a product, a geography, or a customer type) that are incompatible, or not integrated, with other systems in the firm. They added new silos when they introduced new products, new geographies, new customer types, or new service offerings to the existing legacy base (or had to meet new regulations) and left them unconnected. These firms then created *spaghetti* when their point-to point solutions involved making connections from

1-2 Becoming Future Ready

	Integrated Experience	Future Ready
	• Customer gets an integrated experience (simulated) despite complex operations	• Simultaneously innovate and reduce costs
	• Strong design and UX	• Great customer experience
	• Rich mobile experience including purchasing products	• Modular and agile
		• Dynamic partnering
		• Data is a strategic asset
	Silos and Spaghetti	**Industrialized**
	• Product driven	• Plug-and-play products/services
	• Complex landscape of processes, systems, and data	• Service-enabled crown jewels
	• Perform via heroics	• One best way to do each key task
		• Single source of truth

Customer Experience — Increasing customer focus (vertical axis); Transformed

Operational Efficiency ————————————————→ Transformed
Increasing automation, standardization, reuse, and productivity

Source: The future-ready framework and pathways were based on a series of interviews and conversations conducted between 2015 and 2017 on digital transformation with senior executives globally. The framework, pathways, and performance data were quantified in two MIT CISR surveys (2017 and 2019) with further interviews and more than forty workshops between 2018 and 2022.

many systems to many others—particularly when they needed to extract data—with the overall system resembling a plate of spaghetti.

This results in a complex set of business processes, systems, and data supporting their products. The result is a fragmented, labor-intensive, and frustrating experience for both customers and employees, often made worse by product silos. Frequently, the ability of such firms to provide an engaging customer experience depends heavily on heroics by employees. One of us was recently helping her parents with their banking, adding a family member to a checking account and checking the beneficiaries. It required, after several preliminary conversations, getting four of the family members into the same bank branch at the same time, followed by an hour of employee time filling out forms while the family members waited and watched. It was not until another employee in a different unit helped out that these two simple tasks were done. By the end of the ordeal, everyone involved was frustrated. It shouldn't be surprising that the revenue growth and net profit margins of firms in this quadrant were the weakest, averaging 10.5 percentage points and 6.5 percentage points below their industry average (see figure 1-3).

Industrialized

Industrialized firms (bottom right quadrant) focus their initial transformation efforts on applying best engineering practices for automation of their operations. They take the capabilities that made them great as a firm (their crown jewels) and turn them into modular and standardized digitized services. Firms in this group develop the best way of handling each key task (for example, processing an insurance claim, onboarding a customer, assessing risk) and strive to standardize it across the firm. They configure their internal and customer-facing digitized products/services into plug-and-play modules to meet customer needs quickly and inexpensively. They combine data collected from customer interactions and elsewhere to become a single source of truth that anyone with permission in the firm can use in decision-making. Over time, many of these processes and decisions are automated. Only 7 percent of the 1,311 firms were industrialized, and these firms reported average revenue growth of –1.7 percentage points below their industry average and net margins of 2.4 percentage points above the industry average. This mix of superior net margins and slightly below industry average revenue growth reflects the focus

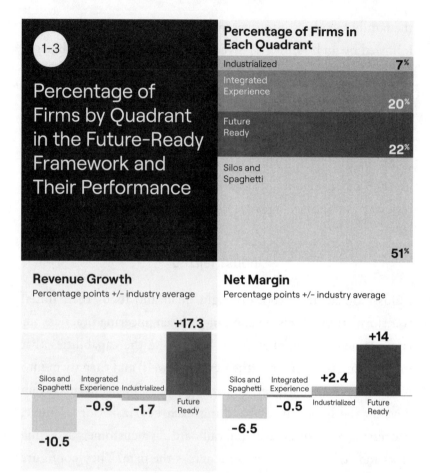

1-3

Percentage of Firms by Quadrant in the Future-Ready Framework and Their Performance

Percentage of Firms in Each Quadrant

Industrialized	**7%**
Integrated Experience	**20%**
Future Ready	**22%**
Silos and Spaghetti	**51%**

Revenue Growth
Percentage points +/– industry average

Silos and Spaghetti **−10.5**
Integrated Experience **−0.9**
Industrialized **−1.7**
Future Ready **+17.3**

Net Margin
Percentage points +/– industry average

Silos and Spaghetti **−6.5**
Integrated Experience **−0.5**
Industrialized **+2.4**
Future Ready **+14**

Source: The future-ready framework and pathways were based on a series of interviews and conversations conducted between 2015 and 2017 on digital transformation with senior executives globally. The framework, pathways, and performance data were quantified in two MIT CISR surveys (2017 and 2019), with further interviews and more than forty workshops between 2018 and 2022. Self-reported net profit margin/revenue growth correlates significantly with actual profit margin/revenue growth at the p<.01 level. Net profit margin and revenue growth are compared to industry and are 5 percent mean trimmed to remove outliers.

on industrialization and operational efficiency of firms in this quadrant.

Integrated Experience

Firms in the integrated experience (top left) quadrant invest in providing a better-than-industry-average customer experience, which they offer despite having complex operations. Firms that want to offer an integrated experience develop attractive websites and mobile apps, and hire designers and more relationship managers to improve the customer experience. Many attempt to improve the customer experience by investing in analytics. However, while improving the customer experience, these integrated experience firms often experience an increased cost to serve the customer as the underlying business processes, technology, and data landscape remains complex or becomes more fragile. About 20 percent of firms are in the integrated experience quadrant and perform around their industry average with average revenue growth of 0.9 and a net margin of 0.5 percentage points below industry average—much improved compared to firms in silos and spaghetti.

Future Ready

Future-ready firms are able to innovate to engage and satisfy customers while at the same time reducing costs. Their goal is typically to meet customers' needs rather than push products, and customers can expect to have a good experience no matter which service delivery channel they choose. On the operations side, the firm's capabilities are modular and agile; data is a strategic asset that is shared and accessible to all in the firm who need it. These firms realize they can't do all of this alone and are organized to leverage partners to add more value to customers.

We found that 22 percent of firms were future ready. These future-ready firms were top performers—with estimated average revenue growth of 17.3 percentage points and a net margin of 14 percentage points above their industry average. An example of a future-ready firm is DBS, considered by many as "the best bank in the world" with both leading customer experience and strong financial

1-4 Future–Ready Framework by Industry

Industry	Silos and Spaghetti	Industrialized	Integrated Experience	Future Ready
Technology	35%	2%	26%	37%
IT Services	42%	3%	30%	26%
Financial Services	56%	7%	13%	24%
Healthcare	60%	3%	14%	23%
Heavy Industry	54%	9%	16%	22%
Manufacturing	48%	11%	19%	22%
Services	51%	6%	23%	20%
Telecom and Media	35%	9%	39%	20%
Consumer	51%	5%	31%	13%
Mining, Oil, and Gas	68%	9%	14%	9%
Not-for-Profit and Government	60%	7%	33%	0%

Source: MIT CISR 2019 Top Management Teams and Transformation Survey (N = 1,311). Industry is self-reported. Industry groupings are based on NAICS coding.

performance, which has transformed to become future ready over the last decade.[7] We will describe DBS's journey in chapter 5.

There are interesting industry differences in the distribution of firms by quadrant (see figure 1-4). For example, the industry with the highest percentage of future-ready firms is technology companies, followed by IT services. The industries with the most firms in the silos and spaghetti quadrant are mining, oil, and gas, not-for-profit and government, healthcare, and financial services (though financial services also have a higher-than-average percentage of firms in future ready). Running your eye down the columns for industrialized and integrated experience gives a quick insight into the direction these industries have moved from silos and spaghetti on their journey to becoming future ready.

We know that almost every firm is exploring how to leverage digital, but we wanted to see if there were differences between the average firm in the sample and small and medium enterprises (SMEs) in their transformations to future ready. There were fewer differences than we expected but some important differences.

We looked at firms in the bottom quartile of annual revenue versus the average firm size. There were many fewer smaller firms in silos and spaghetti (45 percent) than the average (51 percent) and more smaller firms in integrated experience (29 percent vs. 20 percent). There were the same percentage of SMEs in future ready and the average firm (22 percent). Newer, smaller firms are often designed to be future ready.

The Additional Challenge of Large Firms

Many of the firms the MIT Center for Information Systems Research (CISR) works with are very large, with more than $20 billion in annual revenue. We have noticed that moving these very large firms from silos and spaghetti to any other of the quadrants is even more difficult than for the average firm described above. So, we looked at 350 publicly traded firms with average revenue of $29.5 billion, and the results were very sobering. Only 9 percent of these large firms, as opposed to 22 percent of the average firms, had made it to future ready relative to competitors. Around 70 percent of these large firms were in silos and spaghetti compared to 51 percent of the average firms. The good news is that the 9 percent of large firms that made it into future ready were also the top performers.

These very large firms face all the challenges that the average firm encounters in a journey to become future ready plus huge scale and, often, global operations. Creating a clear vision, a common language, culture change, reusable technology platforms, and all the other things needed for transformation is just harder but even more important in these very large companies.

We measure progress toward becoming future ready in a number of ways. For example, we ask senior executives to estimate to what extent they have completed their transformation as proposed to their boards. The answer to this question was 33 percent on average in our 2016 survey and 50 percent in our 2019 survey, with more progress observed in case studies since then—illustrating that the average firm has made slow and steady progress against its promises to the board. But since we assess future-ready firms relative to industry competitors, the bar rises as all firms improve and the performance premiums remain strong.

Progressing to Future Ready

We have identified four pathways that firms can take to become future ready. Each pathway begins in the bottom left quadrant (silos and spaghetti) and involves significant organizational disruption on the way to becoming future ready (see figure 1-5). We will describe these pathways in more detail in later chapters.

Pathway 1: Industrialize

Pathway 1 moves firms from silos and spaghetti toward industrialized. This pathway relies on building a platform mindset with API-enabled (or similar) business services that can be accessed across the enterprise and also externally. It enables a firm to eliminate many of its legacy processes and systems. Pathway 1 also requires putting many other attractive projects on

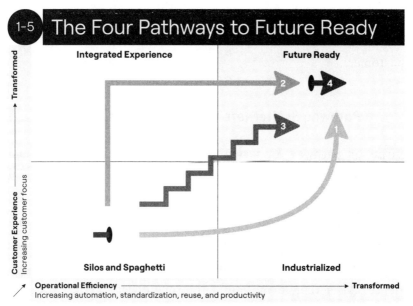

1-5 The Four Pathways to Future Ready

Source: The future-ready framework and pathways were based on a series of interviews and conversations, conducted between 2015 and 2017, on digital transformation with senior executives globally. The framework, pathways, and performance data were quantified in two MIT CISR surveys (2017 and 2019) with further interviews and more than forty workshops between 2018 and 2022.

hold, at least initially. Cloud computing, APIs, microservices, and better solution architectures make this industrialization process quicker, less risky, and less disruptive.[8]

Pathway 2: Delight Customers First

Pathway 2 involves moving from silos and spaghetti toward integrated experience. Firms choose this strategy when their most pressing strategic goal is to improve the customer experience across the whole firm, but they are dealing with multiple organizational silos. Typically, they attempt to do several things at once: develop new attractive offers, build mobile apps and websites, improve customer experience in different channels, and empower relationship managers—all with the goal of delighting the customer. While typically increasing the customer experience, a disadvantage of this pathway is that it initially adds more complexity to already fragmented systems and processes, increasing the cost to serve a customer.

Pathway 3: Alternate the Focus, like Stair Steps

Firms on pathway 3 alternate their focus from improving customer experience to improving operations and then back again, in steady progress to future ready. Firms shift their focus back and forth in shorter efforts—say six months in duration—passing capability and lessons from one step to the next. For example, the first move might be a project to implement an omnichannel experience. After that, firms might improve operations, perhaps by replacing a few legacy processes or creating an API layer. Then, they might attempt to put together a more attractive set of customer offerings by making smarter use of internal data. With this approach, the difference between success and failure is having a road map that informs everyone's efforts versus taking a haphazard approach.

Pathway 4: Create a New Unit

Leaders choose a pathway 4 transformation when it is likely to be an uphill battle to transform the existing firm, or they have a compelling opportunity where success depends on the unit being future ready from the get-go. The advantage of pathway 4 is that it allows an enterprise to build its customer base, people, culture, processes, and systems to be born future ready. It doesn't need to deal with legacy systems or silos or culture change. The challenge is that once the new entity is successful, how does leadership integrate it with the existing firm—or do they?

Multiple Pathways

Which pathway(s) your firm chooses to follow will depend on the competitive position of the firm. We have talked to many large firms where a pathway that is well-suited to one business unit won't work well for another. For example, one business is a leader in customer experience and can focus on pathway 1 to transform, while another business is a laggard on customer experience and needs to follow pathway 2 to remain competitive. Or the firm has a business model innovation it wants to exploit in a new unit (on pathway 4) and, at the same time, needs to transform the existing firm via pathway 3 stair steps. In these cases, it makes sense for a firm to progress on multiple pathways. There's a big caveat, though—firms pursuing multiple pathways must coordinate across the pathways or run the risk of increasing complexity and fragmentation with progress slowing down measurably.

The Four Explosions

Firms have to deal with difficult organizational changes to develop new operational and customer experience capabilities. We call these changes organizational explosions because that's what it feels like when it happens. The changes are significant, disruptive, and affect most of a firm's employees and partners. Some of these explosions are not new, having challenged firms for decades. But when well-managed, these four explosions smooth the way for the journey toward becoming future ready and also create a more agile, digitally savvy, and collaborative culture. For the explosions to create—rather than destroy—value, they need to be addressed carefully, with their impacts anticipated and managed. Explicitly deciding who will and how to manage the explosions typically reduces the time and increases the likelihood of success in becoming future ready. We will describe these explosions in more detail in chapter 2 and show how different firms dealt with them in chapters 3–6.

Future-Ready Capabilities to Develop

To create new types of value, organizations cannot just rely on existing strengths; they must also innovate to leverage powerful, readily accessible technologies. They need to develop ways to adapt their resources and create new capabilities as the environment changes—for example, innovating to accomplish a step-change in performance or acting in response to the moves of competitors, customers, partners, and technologies. Future-ready firms have ten capabilities in common that help create value, enable sustained competitive advantage, and enhance the ability to adapt to what the future brings. In chapter 7, we will describe the capabilities, show how each pathway relies on a different set of capabilities early on, and then provide an assessment so you can evaluate how effectively your firm is building these capabilities.

Value Creation and Capture: Early Indicators of Future-Ready Performance

In the digital era, how firms create and capture value is changing. Operational efficiency and direct customer experience are still critical, but the focus of digital business is shifting to include delivering great digital offerings and creating go-to destinations for customers with partners. This shift is driven by changing customer expectations toward integrated digital experiences that fulfill their more complete needs coupled with digital capabilities making real-time collaboration easier and cheaper. In the world of go-to destinations, firms maximize value by collaborating with partners to increase the size of the opportunities, finding win-win approaches, and sharing the gains rather than relying on the more win-lose approaches from the past.

The key to success in transformations is creating value from digital initiatives, capturing that value in firm performance, and then accumulating that value over time. To help measure progress, we have identified three kinds of value firms create from digital initiatives on the journey to future ready. We will describe the three types here, discuss how some firms created and captured value in chapters 3 through 6, and in chapter 7 discuss how to set up a dashboard to measure the value accumulation along your transformation journey. To know where you are requires two types of measures—those that indicate transformation success by showing what value is captured and those that track effectiveness at building the future-ready capabilities to show how value is created.[9]

Value encompasses all the beneficial outcomes of digital business, like lower cost, better customer experience, more loyalty, and growth from cross-selling and innovative products. Executives described creating three types of digital value (see figure 1-6). Building on these three types, we hypothesize a fourth type, long-term firm value.

1-6 Firms Must Create and Capture Different Kinds of Value

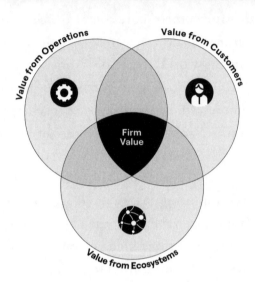

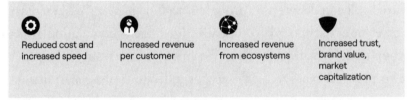

Reduced cost and increased speed	Increased revenue per customer	Increased revenue from ecosystems	Increased trust, brand value, market capitalization

Source: Model is based on twenty-three interviews with executives in 2020. Exploratory statistical analysis with MIT CISR 2019 Top Management Teams and Transformation Survey (N = 1,311). The three sources of value are correlated. Firm value is created when firms are effective at creating the other kinds of value; assessing this value was not part of the current research.

Value from Operations

The foundation of digital business, value from operations, includes reduced cost and increased efficiency and speed. In our research, firms created this value by developing modular components, automating processes, and becoming more open and agile. Firms assessed themselves, on average, as 54 percent effective at creating this value.

Value from Customers

Value from customers encompasses increased revenue from customers via cross-selling and new offerings, plus more customer stickiness and loyalty. Aiding customers to meet their needs, providing a great customer experience, and acting consistently and with purpose helps create this value. Firms can leverage interdependencies between value creation from customers and operations. For example, self-service offerings help create both value from customers and from operations. Creating value from customers is an important predictor of firm success, and firms assessed themselves, on average, as 40 percent effective at creating this value.

Value from Ecosystems

Creating value from ecosystems is often overlooked or deferred, but as firms move to more digitally enabled and partner-based business designs, ecosystem value is becoming more important and a bigger influence on firm performance.[10] Firms create significant value from ecosystems when they leverage partnering to offer go-to destinations, which increase reach (getting more customers) and range (offering more products).[11] Capturing value from ecosystems relies on developing revenues from an ecosystem the firm either leads or participates in and realizing new value from customers and operations through partnering. Firms were, on average, 30 percent effective at creating value from ecosystems.

The three types of accumulated value were significant predictors of firm performance individually. Value from customers had the strongest relative impact; next was value from ecosystems; and finally, value from operations had the least impact. However, value from operations is the scaffolding of digital business, so even if it provides the least direct impact, it is critical to creating and capturing value from customers and ecosystems.

Value from ecosystems contributes only a small part of revenue growth and profitability for the average company today, but we think that ecosystem value in the future will be a significant contributor to company performance for the companies that create it. While many companies are not able to tap the full potential of value from leading ecosystems, by participating in ecosystems and pursuing digital initiatives, they can increase value from ecosystems over time.

We expect that firms that can successfully capture all three types of value and manage the overlap will also create overall longer-term firm value like value from brand, trust, and market capitalization.

Larger firms can learn from SMEs about capturing value, especially value from customers and value from ecosystems. There is no significant difference in how much value from operations SMEs and large firms capture. However, SMEs are better at capturing value from customers and ecosystems than large firms. This is likely because SMEs, being smaller and often local, must be closer to the customer to survive—they typically don't have high brand recognition or large advertising budgets. We hypothesize that SMEs will be more likely to capture value from ecosystems as modular producers,[12] plugging into larger firms' ecosystems to provide specific or local services.

The Structure of the Book

In this chapter, we've set up the framework to become future ready and described the playbook. At the end of this chapter, there is an assessment to help senior executive teams determine where they are on the framework. There is also an exercise to help firm leaders develop a common language—a key enabler of becoming future ready. In subsequent chapters, we describe best practices (from statistical analyses and interviews) and case studies to illustrate how to make progress to becoming future ready. The case studies are designed to share what has worked and help inspire you and your colleagues.

In chapter 2, we describe the four pathways to becoming future ready in detail and what to expect on each pathway. To illustrate the different choices firms make, we describe a firm in financial services following each of the four pathways and one following multiple pathways (pathway 1—Danske Bank; pathway 2—mBank; pathway 3—BBVA; pathway 4—ING; multiple pathways—Bancolombia). We show how BBVA effectively managed the four explosions. We finish with a group exercise to identify the pathway(s) your firm is on and an assessment of how effectively you manage the explosions.

In chapters 3–6, we describe the journey on each of the four pathways in turn with case studies. In chapter 3, we describe the pathway 1 transformations of Kaiser Permanente and Tetra Pak. We conclude with what leaders should focus on—building platforms and innovating rapidly. In chapter 4, we highlight the pathway 2 transformations of CarMax and CEMEX. In a pathway 2 transformation, leaders should focus early on delighting customers and then replatforming. In chapter 5, we look at pathway 3 and the challenges of maintaining progress as the focus alternates between operational efficiency and customer experience; leaders need to focus on synchronizing to ensure progress. Two case studies, DBS and KPN, illustrate success on pathway 3. Chapter 6 is about pathway 4, the creation of new born-digital units—leaders must focus on successfully creating a new business. We use TradeLens and Domain to highlight the opportunities and challenges of creating a new unit. We pose four key questions leaders in firms should ask when building a new born-digital unit (which is like a startup but with a corporate benefactor).

To close the book, in chapter 7, we discuss the role of leaders, including the top management team and the board, in guiding the firm to future ready. To help leaders stay on track on their chosen pathways to becoming future ready, we share a dashboard of value accumulation over time with benchmarks for comparison. We provide an exercise to help you build a dashboard that tracks value and capabilities (the *what* and *how* of value) along the transformation. We finish the book with some musings on what it takes to become future ready and then stay future ready over time.

Assessment: Establish Where Your Firm Is

This self-assessment identifies where your firm is today on the future-ready framework. Rate your firm on a 0 to 100 percent scale on how effective it is on the two axes of the future-ready framework compared to your competitors (see figure 1-7a). Start with assessing operational efficiency, including simplifying processes and services, enabling your core capabilities with APIs, and making them available (internally and externally). You'll rank four critical areas of operational efficiency and then average the four to get a single percentage for operational efficiency. Then do the same with your firm's customer experience, focusing on how effectively, compared to competitors, your firm amplifies the customer voice inside the firm and develops cross-business/

1-7a Future-Ready Framework Assessment

On a scale from 0% (not at all effective) to 100% (very effective),
with 50% the same as your competitors, how effective is your firm at:

Operational Efficiency
(x-axis on the future-ready framework)

Simplifying and automating business processes	%	
Service-enabling core capabilities with APIs	%	Average
Reusing core capabilities and service modules	%	
Measuring productivity and efficiencies	%	

%

Customer Experience
(y-axis on the future-ready framework)

Amplifying the customer voice inside the firm	%	
Developing cross-business/ product customer experiences	%	Average
Defining who can develop new customer offers and experiences	%	
Measuring the effectiveness of customer offers	%	

%

Source: The future-ready framework and pathways were based on a series of interviews and conversations conducted between 2015 and 2017 on digital transformation with senior executives globally. The framework, pathways, and performance data were quantified in two MIT CISR surveys (2017 and 2019) with further interviews and more than forty workshops between 2018 and 2022.

product customer experiences. Finally, plot those ratings on the future-ready framework (see figure 1-7b).

We recommend that you ask multiple colleagues in your firm to complete this assessment independently and then compare the results. You'll get a more complete picture of where your firm is and likely identify divergent assessments in different parts of the firm. Pay attention to the differences, and use them as an opportunity to debate the future of your firm.

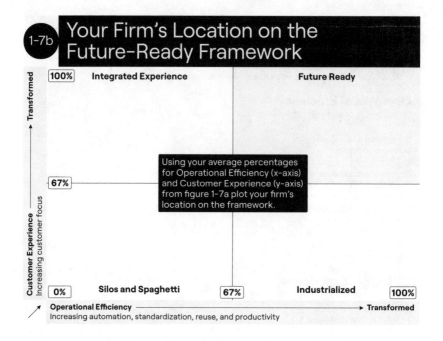

1-7b Your Firm's Location on the Future-Ready Framework

Integrated Experience — 100% (Transformed)

Future Ready

Using your average percentages for Operational Efficiency (x-axis) and Customer Experience (y-axis) from figure 1-7a plot your firm's location on the framework.

67%

Customer Experience — Increasing customer focus

0% — Silos and Spaghetti — 67% — Industrialized — 100%

Operational Efficiency — Transformed — Increasing automation, standardization, reuse, and productivity

Exercise: Develop a Common Language

Using the results from the assessment, let's get the conversation started. One of the exercises we do in our MIT CISR workshops with senior executive teams is to share performance data and examples of firms that are becoming future ready. We then ask the senior management team to break into small groups and discuss what a future-ready version of their firm might look like. This discussion is almost certain to surface conflicting expectations, visions, and even language.

In a recent workshop for the CEO and top management team of a financial services firm, we noticed that the words *platform* and *ecosystem* were used in several different ways by different executives. None of the executives paused to question the meaning and use of the terms. Instead, they were happy with their own words and their unique mindset. The problem was that they were speaking at cross-purposes, which emerged as we facilitated the conversation.

Each executive meant something a little different when using the word *platform*, both around the platform's business purpose and what the platform would look like. The CIO talked about building a platform of digitized services to be used across multiple business-to-consumer (B2C) brands to create efficiency and speed in delivering the firm's current offerings. The CEO described building a new platform business with its own business unit (and profit and loss statement) where they would sell business-to-business (B2B) services to other firms, like payments or identity management. The head of retail talked about building a new self-service retail-only platform to focus on selling traditional banking products like mortgages, loans, and insurance via an app. And the head of the business bank wanted to build a platform to help small businesses thrive and grow and included the bank's products and complementary products from partners like accounting software and customer relationship management (CRM) systems. Upon further discussion, it was clear to all participants that this firm was trying to transform on multiple pathways, but they were not coordinated—not surprising given the lack of common language. Progress was minimal, frustration was high, and there was talk about stopping the transformation because "it will never work."

Using polling when doing workshops helps surface the mindsets and assumptions of every participant: you see the diversity of opinion represented in the polling results instantly. It was this diversity of opinion in polling—on the screen for all to see—that helped the senior executives of this financial services firm realize that they needed to create a common language because they had different assumptions about the platform(s) the bank needed to build, acquire, or rent. If you have to focus on just one of the multiple factors that predict success that we discuss in the book, we'd recommend creating a common language. But developing a common language takes real time and effort—plus constant reinforcement.

Action Items from Chapter 1

1. Position your firm on the 2×2 by completing figure 1-7b to identify the starting point for transformation. There will probably be some disagreement among your team members about where your firm is today. Coming to an agreement about this is important.

2. Discuss whether there is a clear vision for transformation in your firm, driven by its purpose.

3. Set up a time for a conversation among your team members to discuss what a future-ready version of your firm would look like. Ask questions like: What are the capabilities that we need? What do our structure and culture look like? How will we use data? What is our partnering strategy?

4. Start to think about the transformation your firm is currently on (or considering) and identify some of the challenges.

5. Large firms need to use technology to act like a small firm to become more customer-oriented. Think about how to use technology to amplify the customer's voice.

Chapter 2

Four Pathways to Future Ready

Now the fun begins—you know where you are and where you want to go. The next question is how you will get there! After completing the assessment at the end of the last chapter, you and your colleagues know where you are on the framework. Many firms will be in the silos and spaghetti quadrant. And after completing the exercise at the end of chapter 1, you will have a better understanding of what becoming future ready means for your firm and the language you want to use to describe the vision. So, how are you going to get from where you are to your version of future ready? We found four different and viable transformation pathways to future ready (see figure 2-1). Each pathway begins in the bottom left quadrant (silos and spaghetti) and involves significant organizational disruption on the way to becoming future ready.

The choice of a pathway depends on several factors but probably the most important is your competitive position. How urgently do you need to increase your customer experience or improve

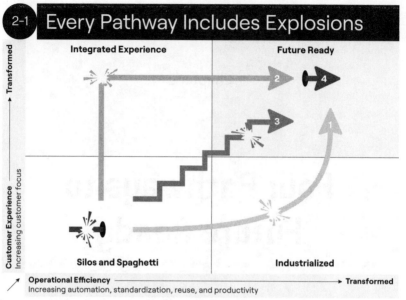

2-1 Every Pathway Includes Explosions

Integrated Experience | Future Ready

Transformed ↑

Customer Experience
Increasing customer focus

Silos and Spaghetti | Industrialized

Operational Efficiency ————————————→ Transformed
Increasing automation, standardization, reuse, and productivity

Note: Explosions on the pathways represent significant organizational changes.

your efficiency? In this chapter, we will describe the pathways, share data on the percentage of firms on each pathway, and explain how far along they are to becoming future ready.

Four Pathway Options

Let's get started by describing each of the four pathways to future ready. We will illustrate each pathway with an example from financial services to show how firms in the same industry can sensibly choose different pathways given their different competitive situations and goals.

Pathway 1: Industrialize

Pathway 1 moves firms from silos and spaghetti to industrialized and then on to future ready, with 25 percent of the firms following this pathway. The goal of pathway 1 is to begin radically simplifying the operations of the firm by focusing on what you're best at—what we call your crown jewels—and turning those into digital services (also referred to as modules). A crown jewel might be your firm's way of onboarding a new customer, processing an insurance claim, designing a new product, writing code, or providing field service—and the associated data. Once those digital services (and their data) have been created, innovation becomes easier and faster by combining modules into new customer offerings. Firms choose this pathway when their customer experience is good enough to hold competitors at bay, and the most pressing strategic goal is to improve operational efficiency. Once efficiency is addressed, they can begin focusing the whole firm on innovating customer offerings by reusing the new modules.

Pathway 1 relies on building a platform that provides reusable and modular digitized business services that can be accessed across the firm and externally by partners. Success requires instilling a platform mindset of silo integration, automation, clean data, and efficiency. Industrialization drives simplification and eliminates many expensive and complex legacy processes and systems first before focusing on product innovation. As anyone who's been through an enterprise resource planning, customer relationship management, or core banking project will attest, it's an expensive multiyear undertaking to rip the core out of a firm and replace it.[1] It also requires putting many other projects on hold. Cloud computing, application programming interfaces (APIs), microservices, better solution architectures, software/product as a service, and agile IT teams make this industrialization process quicker, less risky, and less disruptive than before.[2]

We describe pathway 1 as a hockey stick—shallow at the beginning with hard work and few tangible rewards and becoming much steeper past the midpoint. We call the early parts the "digitization desert." It involves cleanup of legacy systems and data and investments in process simplification and automation. In this difficult period, the CIO, COO, and their operations colleagues ask their line-of-business colleagues to slow down and wait until the early stages of industrialization are completed and the digital processes are ready to use so that they can then innovate quickly, reusing the digitized services like LEGO blocks. During the digitization desert phase, the line-of-business executives feel pressure to perform and typically do not want to wait, so there is often tension and finger-pointing. And this is where firms on pathway 1 fail. Instead of clearly communicating what it will take for all parties in the firm to make progress through the digitization desert to the more exciting part of pathway 1, efforts fragment, with line-of-business leaders creating local solutions for customers while operations leaders continue simplifying and rationalizing. When efforts stall, the CIO or COO is often made the scapegoat.

We have seen firms attempt a pathway 1 transformation several times (the notion of getting all the building blocks in place is attractive), each time with the new CIO or COO leading the charge with the breakthrough technology of the day—only to fail because of demands to locally optimize and meet customer needs. One strategy to make it through the digitization desert is to allocate part of the transformation budget to customer initiatives but require them to be developed as modules that will plug and play and be reused in later stages of the pathway 1 transformation. This is not an easy governance challenge, but it is essential to the success of the transformation toward future ready.

Once the firm is into the steeper part of the transformation hockey stick, transformation becomes a more exciting and fun experience.

New customer offers are launched reusing the plug-and-play digital services created in the first part of the pathway. Processes are faster, cheaper, and simplified. Innovation and efficiency coevolve, and the results are both better customer experience and value from lower cost with industry-leading growth and margins. But reduced costs and simplification must come first on pathway 1.

Danske Bank, headquartered in Copenhagen and operating in sixteen countries in Europe, has a pathway 1 orientation in its DNA. Danske's vision in 2012 was: "One platform—exceptional brands."[3] The focus on operational efficiency and reuse brought some early benefits in the 2000s, for example, a reduction in operating expenses by 20 percent even while acquiring five banks in six years. And this one-platform approach has also delivered longer-term benefits in its relationship with customers and reputation among peers. The bank has reduced the number of branches and has seen tremendous increases in e-banking.[4] Danske's payment app, MobilePay, is so popular today that it has been embraced by over sixty partner banks in the Nordics—a great example of a shared platform.[5]

In 2020, Danske Bank added a strong focus on enhanced customer experience with their Better Bank Transformation strategy.[6] In moving up the steeper part of the pathway 1 hockey stick, the firm is:

- Developing new ways of working with agile transformation projects that respond faster to changing customer expectations, leading to better digital customer experience and reduced costs

- Creating easier day-to-day banking by simplifying product offerings (reducing the number of products by at least 25 percent in 2020) and aligning the portfolio across countries[7]

- Simplifying business unit structures with two business units—Personal & Business Customers and Large Corporates & Institutions

Chris Vogelzang, CEO, Danske Bank, explains:

We continued to make tangible progress in a number of areas, including compliance remediation, societal impact initiatives and new ways of working. This next step will break down silos in our organization and will link directly to the ongoing radical changes to how we work—one of the key initiatives in the Better Bank plan. The combination of a simpler organization and a more agile setup directed towards business development will increase our execution power, achieve a faster time to market and realize synergies across our operations, all aimed at becoming even more competitive for our customers.[8]

Danske's journey is a typical pathway 1 transformation that has moved them toward becoming future ready—where the firm is simultaneously innovating and reducing costs.

Pathway 2: Delight Customers First

Pathway 2 involves moving from silos and spaghetti to the integrated experience quadrant. This transformation is satisfying from day 1. Firms choose this pathway when they are facing pressure from competitors, and their most urgent strategic goal is to improve the customer experience, tackling the problem across multiple organizational silos. Typically, they are driven by local innovation attempting to do several things at once—for instance, develop new attractive offers, build mobile apps and websites, improve call centers, empower relationship managers—all with the goal of measurably increasing customer satisfaction. We found that 18 percent of firms pursued this approach, including many banks, retailers, and energy firms.

The benefit of pathway 2 is that improved customer experience typically leads to higher customer satisfaction scores and increased sales. It's exciting, and every customer-facing part of the business wants to lead its own digital initiatives to improve the customer experience. Once the product or segment leaders taste success in improving the customer experience, they want to do it again— this time, bigger and better. The problem is that the improvements often involve new, stand-alone systems that add more complexity to already complex systems, data, and processes, increasing the cost to serve a customer and challenging employees to perform more heroics to deliver what was promised[9]— switching from one system to another and becoming the concierge for the customer. As firms move along pathway 2, they invest in innovation and new ways of working, like deploying minimum viable products, becoming more evidence-based, and using test-and-learn approaches. To make sure the cost doesn't blow out of control, firms on pathway 2 have to track the cost to serve the customer over time—not an easy task nor done well by many firms.

At some point, the firm must focus on increasing its operational efficiency (moving to the right in this framework) to progress to future ready. Persisting in the transformation and changing the focus (in this case, from customer experience to industrialization) is easier than on pathway 1, as pathway 2 firms have some success with happier customers and increased revenue—and there's momentum to keep going. The problem is that there's no traffic cop saying, "Stop!! Now industrialize!" so the CFO and colleagues play an important role in measuring costs and deciding when the focus needs to shift to industrialization.

Poland's fifth-largest universal banking group, mBank, is an example of a firm that has pursued a pathway 2 transformation.[10] mBank launched its retail banking business as Poland's first digital-only bank in 2000.[11] Leaders realized that the typical banking customer experience in Poland was far from positive. This led to a series of changes, including call centers, online services, and new banking products that increased customer experience. The motto was: "To help. Not to annoy. To delight . . . Anywhere."[12] They focused on innovative offerings, first for the online experience and then for mobile, added in 2012. In 2020, 2.2 million customers of its 4.7 million retail customers used the mobile app.[13]

Shifting its focus to industrialization, in 2014, mBank set out to develop a new banking platform that could provide the flexibility for a continued increase in customer experience. Created over fourteen months, the digital platform offered a wide range of exciting features (including thirty-second loan approvals, mobile payments, video chat, integration with Facebook, peer-to-peer transfers, and cardless ATM withdrawals), and it was designed to increase efficiency and reduce time to market. To grow, mBank then added partners that could tap into its platform and offer more services to its customers—like the French telecom firm Orange S. A. mBank also licensed the platform as "a bank in the box" to noncompeting banks.[14]

In late 2019, mBank launched its new strategy called "Growth Fueled by Our Clients" for 2020 to 2023. With this strategy, mBank continues to advance on pathway 2 while addressing new competition from fintechs and tech firms, as well as new regulations, with four goals: (1) organic customer growth through omnichannel and mobile-first; (2) a retail platform with partners; (3) efficiency through agile teams creating end-to-end solutions, increased automation, and self-service; and (4) employee support through increasing technology and automated tools.[15]

mBank nicely illustrates the journey of pathway 2 as they move toward becoming future ready, navigating a delicate balance of achieving customer, platform, efficiency, and employee goals.

Pathway 3: Alternate the Focus, like Stair Steps

Firms on pathway 3 move toward future ready by alternating the focus of their transformation from improving customer experience to improving operations and then back again, repeating until they reach their goal—with well-defined smaller projects than pathways 1 and 2. For example, the first move might be a project to implement a better omnichannel experience and take six months. After that, firms replace a few legacy processes or create an API layer over another six months. Then, the focus of the transformation may shift to creating a more attractive set of customer offerings that rely on smarter use of customer data for the next eight months of the transformation. We found that 26 percent of firms took the stair-step approach.

With this approach, the difference between success and failure is having a roadmap that informs everyone's efforts (as opposed to a haphazard, less structured approach to project investments). A good way to tell if a firm is disciplined about its pathway 3 transformation is to ask a manager to describe how a specific project fits into the overall plan, especially how coordination between customer experience and operational efficiency initiatives happens.

For many firms, the balanced approach of pathway 3 is an attractive choice because the smaller steps (i.e., the tightly coordinated sets of projects) reduce risk. There are no big bets, and the lessons learned and outputs developed from previous steps can be applied to the next steps. Challenges include governance, inertia, and communication. It's not easy for large organizations to effectively coordinate both transformation projects for customer experience and cost reduction. Setting up successful governance requires clarity on decision rights and accountability—a topic we will return to shortly. Organizational inertia makes it hard to shift direction in large firms, and executives have told us about feeling whiplash as they move from focusing on costs to focusing on customer experience and back again. Communicating those changes can be difficult and even confusing to employees, markets, and customers. Even more challenging is taking the benefits from each step and passing them on to the next project. When pathway 3 is not going smoothly, the steps don't connect, so the firm doesn't get cumulative benefits.

Banco Bilbao Vizcaya Argentaria S. A. (BBVA), a large international bank headquartered in Bilbao, Spain, took pathway 3 to digitally transform. To improve efficiency, BBVA worked hard to remove the spaghetti-like business processes that had been constructed over time from many different systems and versions of data, replacing them with scalable, reusable global digital platforms. Then, in its effort to reshape the customer experience, BBVA positioned its mobile app, introduced in 2014, as a remote-control device for banking customers. The mobile app offered simple new customer onboarding in less than five minutes, plus most product purchases in under a minute. Customers had a self-service suite of products, including consumer loans and investment funds. It was also a digital wallet and allowed customers to set up appointments and conduct messaging with managers.

As BBVA progressed along its digital transformation, the alternating stair steps, improving operational efficiency and customer experience capabilities, became synergistic so that BBVA eventually was able to work on both dimensions more in parallel, with connected digital initiatives that were tightly coordinated. Today, BBVA offers customers a digital experience via a reliable core banking platform, enabling new developments that combine the bank's open APIs and other capabilities. A big advantage of this approach is that other firms, including retailers, telcos, and even startups, are able to tie into the bank's services, thereby enhancing their own products.

In 2019, BBVA had the number one net-promoter score in most of its markets.[16] By 2020, digital and mobile customers made up 60 percent and 56 percent of their customer base, respectively.[17] Digital sales were 66 percent of total sales, and for the first time, the value of digital sales exceeded the value of transactions from other channels.[18]

To increase coordination, CEO (now executive chairman) Carlos Torres wanted to make sure people were being assigned to initiatives that would have the biggest strategic impact rather than simply the largest budget. BBVA launched an investment process called the single development agenda (SDA). SDA leveraged the cadence of agile development to learn from, evaluate, and prioritize more than two thousand initiatives each quarter. Each initiative has to report what they have delivered and the value they have created and must estimate the talent needed for the next quarter. The SDA process has helped BBVA invest a greater percentage of its total initiative spending on strategic priorities (allocating 75 percent to strategic initiatives in 2021, up from 60 percent in 2018), and it has helped initiatives generate value faster (taking 1.9 years to realize value in 2018, dropping to 1.4 years in 2021).[19]

BBVA's journey is typical for a pathway 3 transformation, especially one that has been ongoing, as the cost and customer experience initiatives become more interconnected. Pathway 3 is a good choice for firms that need to quickly improve both customer experience and operational efficiency and are willing and able to apply the governance discipline to make it work.

Pathway 4: Create a New Unit

Senior leaders choose pathway 4 when they believe transforming their current firm will take too long and will require a very different culture, skills, and systems than exist today. Rather than struggle with the existing organization, leaders start new firms or business units that begin life future ready. Some firms also choose a pathway 4 transformation when they have an exciting opportunity that can't be accomplished by leveraging their current capabilities, brand, or regulatory environment. We found that 7 percent of firms chose this pathway as their dominant transformation strategy. For example, Audi AG, the German car firm, created a "born-digital" subsidiary to develop mobility services. Toyota and BMW have taken similar approaches.

Pathway 4 allows a firm to build its customer base, people, culture, processes, and systems from scratch to be future ready. It doesn't need to deal with legacy systems or culture or organizational silos. One challenge of the pathway 4 approach is that firms create a new cool organization, which may become the focus of attention and investment while the traditional organization trudges along. Perhaps the greatest challenge is that once the new entity is successful, how do you—or *do* you—integrate it with the parent organization?

The ING Group, the multinational banking and financial services firm based in Amsterdam, pursued a pathway 4 approach more than two decades ago with ING Direct. ING launched ING Direct first in Canada in 1997 before expanding into Australia, Italy, Spain, the United Kingdom, the United States, and other countries. The transformation strategy was to pioneer a direct banking model in new markets.[20] Although ING Direct did have some ATMs, it had no branches. Customers interacted with the bank by phone, mail, or internet. After beginning as a low-cost bank offering high-interest deposit products, it gradually added new products like loans and mortgages. By 2006, it had 13 million customers in nine countries.[21]

ING Direct's country-based businesses operated autonomously but shared a common set of standardized business solutions and technical platform components. The reuse of modules and components kept operational costs low (at 0.43 percent of assets as compared to 2.5 percent of assets for a typical full-service bank), allowing the businesses to offer higher savings rates and lower-cost loans.[22]

In 2008, ING added another component to its digital transformation—digitizing its branch model. By transforming from physical to digital operations, the parent firm reduced the number of branches from 600 to 260 in the Netherlands while decreasing the time to open an account from twenty days to twenty minutes. In 2014, the firm was ready to start bringing ING Direct back in with the new strategic goal of creating one global platform and one ING experience.[23] But there was no single ING Direct—each country operated a little differently. ING integrated ING Direct, creating a high-profile marketing campaign around renaming to ING in some markets (e.g., Australia and Spain), while it sold its ING Direct units in other markets (i.e., United States, United Kingdom, and Canada).[24]

ING Direct gives us a unique window into pathway 4—twenty years on. ING Direct arguably changed banking expectations for its customers and competitors and lowered its cost to serve worldwide, but it wasn't easy to manage both the ING and ING Direct business models in one firm, given their different leaders, platforms, culture, and business models. Today, driven by a plethora of neo-banks and digital banks started in the last few years, we are seeing many traditional financial services firms using a pathway 4 approach to compete and move quickly. Digital banks recently started by traditional banks are slowly and steadily gathering momentum, customer base, and profits. They include next by Bradesco in Brazil, Openbank by Santander in Europe, Nequi by Bancolombia in Colombia, and UBank by National Australia Bank. The big question is: How will these new digital banks, all pathway 4 initiatives, capture the value they create? And how will they operate—as separate entities (maybe even becoming public) or as new platforms in the existing firms to support current customers? Or will they get integrated into the parent firm?

Choosing a Pathway

Leadership's role is to determine which pathway(s) the firm (or unit) should take and how aggressively to move. Leaders need to start by assessing, honestly, where the firm is today (based on metrics such as net-promoter score and net margin) compared to the rest of the industry (the future-ready assessment in the previous chapter is a good first step). Then, the choice of pathway will depend on the firm's circumstances, the competitive environment, and the direction management thinks best fits the firm's current capabilities:[25]

- Pathway 1 makes sense if the firm's customer experience is around the industry average and the threat of digital disruption is not high. CIOs are a good choice to lead pathway 1.

- Pathway 2 makes sense if the firm's customer experience is significantly worse than average and you can't wait to improve or there are scary new competitors. An executive passionate about customer experience who is digitally savvy would be a good choice to lead pathway 2.

- Pathway 3 makes sense if the firm's customer experience is not leading, but senior leaders can identify a few initiatives that will make a big difference. They start with those, then focus on operations, and repeat in small steps. A chief digital officer that gets both customer experience and operations would be a good choice to lead pathway 3.

- Pathway 4—building a new firm or business unit—makes sense when leadership can't see a way to change the culture or the customer experience and operations in the firm fast enough to survive or to take advantage of an opportunity. The firm's CEO, who usually appoints a leader for a new unit, would be a good choice to lead pathway 4.

Once the firm—that is, the board, the CEO, and the senior management team—settles on a pathway, the difficult work

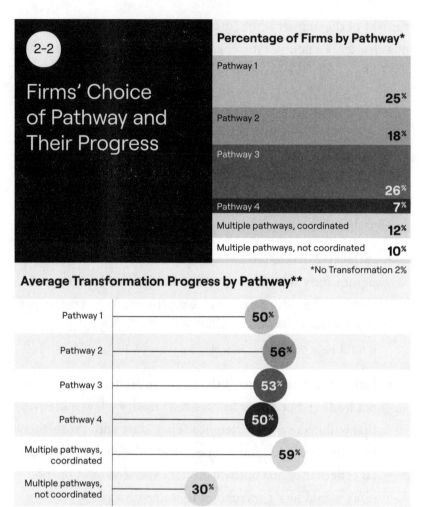

2-2

Firms' Choice of Pathway and Their Progress

Percentage of Firms by Pathway*

Pathway 1 — **25%**

Pathway 2 — **18%**

Pathway 3 — **26%**

Pathway 4 — **7%**

Multiple pathways, coordinated — **12%**

Multiple pathways, not coordinated — **10%**

*No Transformation 2%

Average Transformation Progress by Pathway**

Pathway 1 — **50%**

Pathway 2 — **56%**

Pathway 3 — **53%**

Pathway 4 — **50%**

Multiple pathways, coordinated — **59%**

Multiple pathways, not coordinated — **30%**

Source: The future-ready framework and pathways were based on a series of interviews and conversations, conducted between 2015 and 2017, on digital transformation with senior executives globally. The framework, pathways, and performance data were quantified in two MIT CISR surveys (2017 and 2019) with further interviews and more than forty workshops between 2018 and 2022. **Average transformation progress is the average of firms' estimates of pathway completion based on what was proposed to the board or CEO.

begins—completing the transformation. Figure 2-2 shows the percentage of firms following each pathway and their progress toward transformation (relative to what was proposed by the executive team to the board). Interestingly, 78 percent of the 1,311 firms surveyed chose one primary pathway for their digital transformation, even though many were large firms. SMEs are less likely to be on multiple pathways, either coordinated or not, and the scale of their transformation within the firm is less than that of large firms.

In late 2019, firms had, on average, progressed to 50 percent complete on their transformations compared to 33 percent in 2017. Fifty percent complete is an important milestone for value creation. We found that firms that were above 50 percent complete in their transformations had a 14 percent higher average net margin (adjusted for industry) than those below 50 percent complete.

Multiple Pathways

Of the 22 percent of firms that chose multiple pathways, more than half (12 percent of total firms) said they were well-coordinated. These firms had made the most progress: their transformations were, on average, 59 percent complete. In contrast, the firms that pursued multiple uncoordinated pathways made the least progress—30 percent complete. One risk we see in the next few years is that business units or country or product leaders will drive local transformation initiatives after being frustrated with slow progress on firm-wide transformation. The firm will then be on multiple uncoordinated pathways, and the financial results will be poor, as future ready remains out of reach.

One firm that is on multiple well-coordinated pathways is Bancolombia,[26] the largest commercial bank in Colombia and one of the largest in Latin America, with 2021 revenues of $1.1 billion.[27] Bancolombia provides a range of financial products and services to both individual and corporate customers.

Bancolombia followed a pathway 3 transformation, moving back and forth between focusing on customer experience and operational efficiency to become future ready. The firm also created a new digital bank, Nequi, anticipating the entry of new players in its region, a pathway 4 approach.

Nequi came out of Bancolombia's innovation lab and operated like a startup. It was part of the Bancolombia group and had a life of its own, with 10 million active users in 2021.[28] At the same time, Bancolombia continually evaluated its risks and opportunities. Nequi's success stemmed from its user focus, reinvention capacity, and high resilience. Its business model, as well as its skills, technology, operating model, and working culture, differed significantly from the parent firm. Nequi built its technological infrastructure in the cloud, separated from Bancolombia's infrastructure, and integrated it to Bancolombia through the bank's accounting systems.

External auditors recommended that Nequi's team follow the same strict, standard processes as traditional banks. However, Nequi created a different culture that translated into speed and new products. Bancolombia designed Nequi as a test laboratory for technology—with Nequi testing technologies like authentication through face and voice recognition, new ways of working, and product development. Nequi used self-organizing, cross-functional agile teams intuitively as part of their working culture, which helped create functionalities faster. In product development, Bancolombia tested financial and nonfinancial businesses through Nequi by experimenting with external APIs to develop an open ecosystem.

Nequi had multiple connections with its parent firm. Its customers could use Bancolombia's 6,000 ATMs and 21,000 non-bank correspondents[29] to make financial transactions. Money was passed between Bancolombia and Nequi in realtime without going through payment networks. We'll come back to Bancolombia and Nequi, and what eventually happened to Nequi, in chapter 6.

Being on multiple pathways makes sense for many large firms, but it requires even more coordination and sharing of best practices and digital services like customer data across the different pathways. BankCo, the bank we described in chapter 1, followed three pathways, reasonably well-coordinated. Pathway 1 was the primary pathway, accounting for 70 percent of their transformation spend and focusing on simplifying legacy systems and processes to create an efficient mortgage engine that could support both direct sales and sales through partners. The bank also pursued pathway 2. About 20 percent of their transformation spend was allocated to customer-experience-focused projects to keep the bank competitive in the marketplace. Ten percent was allocated to creating an ecosystem for homeownership with complimentary products for customers provided by partners like insurance, legal services, and brokers to help with finding and buying properties.

In reviewing statistically what makes a difference in managing a transformation with multiple pathways, firms that have made the most progress in their transformation perform three activities really well. These firms:[30]

1. **Develop a coach-and-communication orientation:** A multiple-pathways transformation is typically just too complex to manage centrally and requires every person's active involvement and creativity. To succeed, firms have to move away from a command-and-control management style and communicate the vision and plan, and coach on how to succeed.

2. **Focus on a cross-product customer experience:** Product integration is hard, and successful customer solutions often involve integrating products and services from multiple business units. Pursuing multiple transformations among the different business units makes creating a cross-product experience even harder (think about how the new product and service modules need to work together) and therefore needs special attention and coordination—perhaps by a head of customer experience. Specifically focusing on a cross-product experience ensures coordination will be top-of-mind, making it more likely that customers will enjoy a more seamless experience.

3. **Leverage innovation:** Transforming on multiple pathways, while more complicated, also increases the opportunity to leverage innovations, as there are more places that innovations can be applied (and reused). Leaders who can solve the coordination issues of being on multiple pathways get more value from innovation.

Value Accumulates Differently, but All Pathways Pay Off

The good news is that all four pathways lead to success. The more firms progress on their transformations, the better the growth and margin benefits. But measuring firm growth and margin in real time and attributing these metrics to transformation progress is very difficult, as firm performance often lags and is impacted by many factors.

To understand how firms accumulate value along the digital transformation journey, we use the three types of value firms create from digital initiatives introduced in chapter 1—value from operations, value from customers, and value from ecosystems. In chapters 3 to 6, we will identify which types of value to focus on early in your transformation, based on your choice of pathway, and describe how firms we studied build capabilities and manage the four explosions we introduced in chapter 1. In chapter 7, we will introduce a dashboard with metrics and benchmarks, breaking down the transformation into thirds so you can track and compare the value you accumulate over time. The dashboard includes two important components—*what* value is created from digital (value from operations, value from customers, and value from ecosystems) and *how* is value created (via ten future-ready capabilities in four areas: operational, customer, ecosystem, and foundational).

As firms progress on their digital transformation, they increase the value accumulated from operations, customers, and ecosystems. The steady increase in all three types of value shows how successful transformations build skills and capabilities over time that result in measurable improvements. Value from operations accumulates most rapidly, followed by value from customers, and finally, value from ecosystems. To make sure your firm is progressing on its transformation, you need a measurement dashboard that shows everyone how value accumulates in these three areas. For example, BankCo, mentioned above, created a dashboard with three or four metrics for each type of value and tracked their progress over time, reporting regularly to the board. That dashboard was also available to employees. A helpful exercise is to identify three to four metrics (no more!) for each of the operations, customers, and ecosystems, so you can all agree on the important signposts for the success of your transformation. To get your conversation started, here are the metrics we used to measure progress on accumulating value:

- **Value from Operations**: Effectiveness of your firm's cost of operations, speed to market, and operational efficiency, compared to competitors.

- **Value from Customers**: The percentage of your firm's revenue from cross-selling, the percentage of your firm's revenue from new products, and the effectiveness of your firm's efforts at generating customer stickiness (i.e., retention and use).

- **Value from Ecosystems**: The percentage of your firm's revenue coming from ecosystems, the effectiveness of your firm's efforts to create bundled products and services with partners, and the percentage of the ecosystem data your firm has access to.

The Four Explosions

Becoming future ready is hard work. Large firms have typically developed a wide range of products and services over many years, supported by an ingrained and nondigital culture. These products and services are often organized in silos that are interconnected by a complex web of processes, practices, systems, and data. This complexity makes it hard for employees to deliver value, resulting in a fragmented and frustrating experience for customers. In studying digital business transformations, we identified four significant, disruptive changes leaders have to make to develop the new operational and customer experience capabilities that will

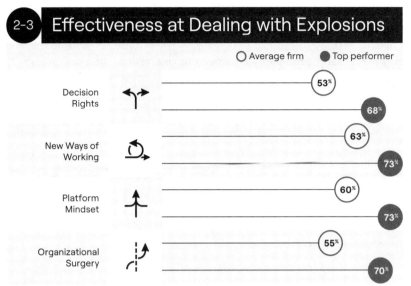

2-3 Effectiveness at Dealing with Explosions

○ Average firm ● Top performer

Decision Rights
53%
68%

New Ways of Working
63%
73%

Platform Mindset
60%
73%

Organizational Surgery
55%
70%

Source: MIT CISR 2019 Top Management Teams and Transformation Survey (N = 1,311). Top performers are the top quartile of firms on net margin, adjusted for industry. Self reported net profit margin correlates significantly with actual profit margin at the p<.01 level.

help overcome the complexity and move the firm toward future ready. We call these four changes explosions because that's how they feel—firms are blowing up the way they used to do things to remove barriers and move faster. Each firm experiences the explosions slightly differently, depending on its capabilities, competitive landscape, industry regulations, strategic goals, and other firm characteristics. Explicitly discussing how to anticipate and manage the explosions helps keep firms focused on enabling their transformations. Top performers were around 70 percent more effective at managing all four explosions than the average firm (see figure 2-3). How does your firm compare?

Decision Rights

Transformations change the status quo of who makes and is held accountable for key decisions, such as when a key process is formally changed, which projects receive funding, and which products are discontinued and launched. Specifying decision rights has long been a key component of effective IT governance,[31] but in the digital era, it extends beyond the IT department to the visioning, provisioning, and use of digital technology throughout the firm. There are only a few key decision rights that typically need attention. For example, separating the decision rights between what needs to be done versus how it will be delivered is key to developing agility. Giving the "what to do" and "how to do it" decision rights to a single group will likely keep the firm mired in silos and spaghetti.

New Ways of Working

Improving both customer experience and operational efficiency requires rethinking and redesigning the way employees work, and it is an opportunity to empower and excite your people with new challenges and successes. New ways of working often include cocreating products and services with customers, developing new partnerships that speed time to market, engaging in test-and-learn experimentation, building more evidence-based behaviors, and working more collaboratively in cross-functional teams using agile approaches.

Platform Mindset

Becoming future ready requires learning from platform firms like Amazon, PayPal, and WeChat and developing a platform mindset. Creating a platform mindset is about recognizing that reusable digital services enable the firm to innovate and scale its operations and offerings faster.[32] Firms take what makes them great and turn them into digital services that are modular, service-enabled, and reusable. They work on their fragmented systems by integrating their silos, standardizing their processes, and automating where possible.

Organizational Surgery

Also known as restructuring or reorganization, these organizational design changes remove organizational complexity and help the firm focus on better customer offerings. Most firms have gone through different forms of organizational surgery for decades—it helps prevent inertia, can reduce the cost base, and supports strategic direction changes in the face of major industry transformation.[33] In the transformation to becoming future ready, firms typically recognize that the way they are organized today is not best-suited for their desired new ways of operating, and some kind of organizational surgery is needed. The surgery typically involves reworking business processes to better support customer journeys, integrating firm silos, and (more recently) the flattening of hierarchies, along with corresponding revisions of functional roles, reporting lines, and incentives to speed up.

Explicitly deciding who will and how to manage the explosions typically reduces the time and increases the likely success of becoming future ready.

BBVA's Management of Explosions

Now, we will return to BBVA and reflect briefly (see figure 2-4) on how the bank has handled the four explosions during its ongoing transformation. The goal is to help you think about the

2-4 How BBVA Dealt with Explosions

⚕ Decision Rights

- Identified five key areas (e.g., talent and culture, engineering, customer solutions) and installed leadership from inside and outside the firm

- Separated the decision rights of the go-to market strategy and delivery execution

- Created the SDA process for prioritization, value identification, coordination, and resourcing of all projects

⚕ New Ways of Working

- Embraced agile methods, creating hundreds of multidisciplinary scrum teams

- Oriented work around the customer voice—e.g., cataloging customer journeys as the basis for proactive and personalized advice, positioning the mobile app as the primary customer touchpoint

⚕ Platform Mindset

- Replaced IT spaghetti with scalable, standardized platforms that combined optimized business processes, efficient technology, and accessible data

- Invested in internal and external API initiatives

⚕ Organizational Surgery

- Combined groups serving and selling to customers into one group, execution and performance

- Combined operations, IT, and some products to create a new engineering core competency providing firm-wide banking services

- Established a subsidiary data group to partner with units on monetizing data

Source: Interviews with company executives; company documents.

kind of changes you need to make to drive new capabilities and value creation.

By 2013 BBVA's Francisco González, then executive chairman of the bank, had been worried for some time. BBVA needed to act increasingly swiftly and decisively to meet changing customer behavior. Banking was facing imminent digital disruption, and González feared that customers would start to take up less of

BBVA's services in favor of more innovative financial services offered by fintech startups and the internet giants. González articulated the vision, "We are building the best digital bank of the 21st century."[34]

Platform Mindset

Fortunately, BBVA had already laid a lot of the groundwork around platforms. It had always been a tech-savvy bank, investing heavily in reusable global platforms since 2007 to compete in more than thirty countries serving 71 million customers. The bank worked hard at untangling its partly digitized business processes, and, at the same time, it started to replace those old processes and systems with more efficient and scalable global digital platforms. Those platforms were designed to combine optimized business processes, efficient technology, and accessible data—all at a lower cost than incurred by industry competitors. This platform mindset was one of the enablers for BBVA's mobile app—named the best mobile banking app in the world for three consecutive years by Forrester Research.[35] One good way to assess the effectiveness of a firm's platform mindset is to look at the cost to income ratio. BBVA's ratio was 46.8 in December 2020, decreasing and below the industry average (63.7 percent).[36]

Decision Rights and Organizational Surgery

In 2014/2015, BBVA announced radical organizational surgery to move the bank another step closer to González's vision of a digital bank. Carlos Torres Vila, who was appointed head of the new Digital Banking unit in 2014, was named CEO, and the bank was reorganized to smooth the move to digital. A new unit, Execution and Performance, combined the groups focused on serving customers and selling. The new engineering core competency combined operations, IT, and some products to provide firm-wide banking services. As part of this transformation, the bank looked outside for leaders, particularly in the new core competency areas, and several came from outside the banking industry.

BBVA has continued to introduce new structures to help create value and drive its transformation progress. For example, BBVA established the subsidiary BBVA Data & Analytics in 2014 to help monetize their data. The group was tasked to be the go-to place for BBVA's data capability, a community of experts that work with the business leaders on data projects. By the end of 2017, Data & Analytics had launched more than forty data science projects for one-third of BBVA's business units, some of which led to new digital offerings. BBVA also established a data office that reported to the CEO, recognizing data as a core competency.[37] The recent introduction of the SDA process for prioritization, value identification, coordination, and resourcing of all projects gave the bank a single view of their innovation efforts, further clarifying decision rights.

New Ways of Working

BBVA adopted fresh approaches to getting work done. For example, it embraced agile methods at scale. Hundreds of multidisciplinary, dedicated scrum teams worked together to develop new features in two-week sprints, with quarterly planning to ensure systematic, accountable, and transparent project management. The bank overhauled the culture and embraced new cultural values (like a test-and-learn mentality and empowerment through accountability) with two goals—attract and retain the best and most needed talent and create a more agile and enterprising corporate culture.

In June 2021, BBVA described its transformation journey to a digital, data-driven bank in four steps: (1) serve customers digitally; (2) increase digital sales; (3) increase reach (add more customers) digitally; and (4) provide proactive and personalized advice. The bank is working on step 4. For example, it has created a Global Journeys Catalog with about fifty journeys to advise customers on four objectives: controlling day-to-day income and expenses, managing debt, building a safety net, and planning.[38]

Throughout its journey, BBVA has learned several important lessons, including that the leaders must get the entire organization, including every person in the branch network, onboard. Every employee has to play a role in creating the new digitally transformed firm. Most important, employees need to feel like part of the team and believe that their contributions matter.

In our workshops and presentations, we are often asked which of these explosions should be dealt with first. Our analysis of case vignettes and survey data suggests that no matter which pathway you are on, the first explosion to focus on is decision rights. We hear of many firms starting their transformation with organizational surgery—often prematurely before really understanding the problems they need to fix. Instead, we find that clarifying who is responsible for the key decisions in digital, like investment prioritization, new customer offers, or one way of doing key tasks like customer onboarding, is the best place to start.

In chapters 3 to 6, we will discuss each pathway, in turn, going into detail about the journey. We will expand on how firms have been successfully managing the explosions and in what order, and making progress toward future ready.

We conclude on a cautionary but realistic note. We recently ran a workshop on digital business transformation with the CEO and the top executive team of a large financial services firm. We asked each attendee to plot their firm's transformation over the previous three years using the pathways framework. After the other executives had presented several different versions of the firm's transformation, we invited the CEO to share his version. He drew a series of movements, beginning at silos and spaghetti, moving up, then to the right, then down and back, charting a convoluted path that continued for several more squiggles. When the CEO finished, he stepped back and said, "You know, it's not as if we planned to do it that way. But using the objective metrics against our industry, this is the path we followed."

He concluded by expressing his view that leaders need to adopt a common language, pick a pathway, and then stick to it (unless circumstances radically change), and they all agreed. We think this is very good advice. After all, business transformation is difficult. In every firm, all stakeholders (including the board, employees, partners, and customers) need to know where the firm is going and how it will get there—even more important when the inevitable setbacks occur.

The digital era is a great opportunity for leaders to reinvent the firm. The most successful firms will become future ready, developing ambidexterity and constantly innovating to improve the customer experience while also reducing costs. Those that don't become future ready will likely suffer a death by a thousand cuts, with startups, players from other industries, and agile competitors slicing bits out of their businesses.

Exercise: Choosing a Pathway

Bring a group together that represents the entire firm. We typically do this exercise with the CEO and the top leadership team. Using the assessment (see figure 2-5), ask every participant independently to identify which pathway or pathways the firm is pursuing. There are seven choices. Each executive can choose pathways 1 to 4 or multiple well-coordinated pathways or multiple uncoordinated

2-5 Pathways Assessment

Choose the approach that best describes your firm's approach to digital business transformation (choose one).

My firm's transformation is:

○ **Path 1**: Focused on improving our operational efficiency capabilities first, before improving our customer experience capabilities

○ **Path 2**: Focused on improving our customer experience capabilities first, before improving our operational efficiency capabilities

○ **Path 3**: Incremental, alternately focusing on improving customer experience and operational efficiency

○ **Path 4**: Creating a new company/unit designed to succeed in the digital economy

○ Following more than one of these paths, **well-coordinated**

○ Following more than one of these paths, but **not well-coordinated**

○ We are not undergoing or have not started a transformation

How far along is your firm on its digital business transformation (i.e., percentage complete) based on what was proposed to the board or CEO?

Estimate the percentage complete:
(0%—we haven't started yet, 100%—we are done)

%

Source: The future-ready framework and pathways were based on a series of interviews and conversations conducted between 2015 and 2017 on digital transformation with senior executives globally. The framework, pathways, and performance data were quantified in two MIT CISR surveys (2017 and 2019) with further interviews and more than forty workshops between 2018 and 2022.

pathways. Plus, we added "no transformation" as an option. If people choose that, an interesting conversation will likely follow. If the firm is on a transformation pathway, estimate how far along it is on its digital transformation (the percent complete) compared to the plan that was proposed to the board or CEO. Once you have all voted (this is another exercise where using an online polling tool works great) and shared your results, break into pairs. Each person in the pair has to explain her answer to the other person—so practice your arguments. Continuing on, share your thoughts on how far your firm has progressed and the roadblocks you face. Then, come together as a group and talk through the differences and whether the firm should change pathways. Typically, there is a wide variation of responses reflecting different assumptions held in the minds of participants. These are important to discuss, which will also lead to more of a common language. Have fun, and strive to reach consensus—your firm's future will depend on it.

Assessment: Explosions

Once you have achieved consensus on which pathway(s) to follow toward future ready, it's time to tackle the explosions. We have found that a good place to start is to do polling about how effective your firm is today at managing each explosion (see figure 2-6). Then, have a conversation in breakout groups about which explosion(s) you should focus on next and what's one big, bold recommendation you would like the CEO to implement to manage the explosion effectively.

2-6 Explosions Assessment

How effective is your firm at:	Not at all effective 0%	Slightly effective 25%	Moderately effective 50%	Very effective 75%	Extremely effective 100%
Changing decision rights?	◯	◯	◯	◯	◯
Developing new ways of working (e.g., agile, test and learn)?	◯	◯	◯	◯	◯
Instilling a mindset around creating and reusing platforms?	◯	◯	◯	◯	◯
Restructuring the firm?	◯	◯	◯	◯	◯

Source: The future-ready framework and pathways were based on a series of interviews and conversations conducted between 2015 and 2017 on digital transformation with senior executives globally. The framework, pathways, and performance data were quantified in two MIT CISR surveys (2017 and 2019) with further interviews and more than forty workshops between 2018 and 2022.

Action Items from Chapter 2

1. Choose a pathway(s) to become future ready in a way that involves the right people and gains commitment. The key is to have the right people contributing to the decision, using a common shared language, and leaving with a commitment to drive the transformation.

2. Create a plan for getting out in front of the explosions— those inevitable disruptions. For example, identifying what three or four key decision rights you have to change is a great place to start.

3. This is a good time to start to think about who is going to lead the transformation and how you will measure value. Plus, leaders have to identify the activities that will be

stopped to free up time, attention, and budget for the proposed transformation.

4. Create a communication plan across the organization to
   share the upcoming future-ready journey and what the
   firm's leaders expect of everyone to help make it successful.
   You need buy-in from the entire firm!

Chapter 3

Pathway 1

Industrialize

We now begin the first of four chapters that discuss the journey for each of the four pathways. This chapter covers pathway 1—industrialization. This pathway is about building digital operational strength first and then using that strength to rapidly innovate and delight customers. We describe two distinct phases of pathway 1 and discuss the leadership practices and mechanisms that enable firms to move more quickly. We learn from case studies of Kaiser Permanente and Tetra Pak how to make progress along pathway 1 and how to deal with the organizational explosions. We finish with a to-do list for leaders.

Why Follow Pathway 1 and What to Expect

In our latest survey,[1] around 25 percent of firms across all industries adopt pathway 1. These firms typically have a good enough customer experience and perceive the lowest (but still significant) level of revenues under threat from digital disruption in the next five years—they estimate 26 percent of their revenues will be lost if they don't change.[2] The lower level of threat is important because pathway 1 has two phases: the handle and the hook of the hockey stick. These two phases are building platform capabilities (the handle) and then exploiting those capabilities with rapid innovation (the hook). Building the capabilities takes time, and if the firm is well behind in customer experience, they often can't afford to follow pathway 1 alone.

There are interesting industry differences among firms picking pathway 1. For example, 35 percent of manufacturing and heavy industry firms in our latest survey[3] pick this pathway—well above average—focusing on operational excellence is a comfortable approach to digital for these firms. In contrast, only 16 percent of education, not-for-profit, and government enterprises pick pathway 1, with similar percentages for banking and insurance firms. The technology industry has the highest percentage of firms picking pathway 1, with 42 percent of firms pursuing this pathway, typically (re)building a series of platforms first and then exploiting them by creating new and better customer offers.

Firms typically pick pathway 1 when they have time to build new capabilities to simplify and reduce the cost to serve customers. Although platforms have technical definitions, our simplistic way to think about platforms is that you take what you're great at—your crown jewels—*what you (will) do better than anyone else*—and turn them into reliable, low-cost, standardized, and reusable digital services that can be combined quickly into new or existing digital offerings for customers either by your firm or by partners. The platform is an integrated set of digitized business processes and the technologies, service modules, compliance checks, and data to achieve a specific purpose (like taking an order). Not all business processes are digitized, at least initially. Some require human intervention, but the goal is to fully automate them. And not all digitized processes are part of a single platform—the platform integrates a set of related processes and transactions. At some firms, the platform is anchored in a major piece of purchased software, such as an enterprise resource planning system or a customer relationship management system. More recently, firms can develop their platform(s) in the cloud or acquire (or use for a fee) systems offered by other firms in the cloud. People (or other systems) provide input to a digitized platform and can use the output, but people are not part of the platform itself. The purpose of a platform is to disengage people from processes that are better performed by machines. The platform "wires" reliable, predictable, low-cost core business transactions into the firm, enabling both self-service and curated service.[4] More recently, artificial intelligence (AI) has helped firms develop their platforms to make (or recommend) more decisions. For example, the Australian Tax Office created an AI solution that nudged taxpayers toward productive tax claim behaviors in real time, which resulted in $113 million in changed claim amounts in 2018.[5]

A platform captures the essence of a firm's strategy and digitizes its crown jewels into a modular and reusable set of services. In building the new platforms, firms must first decide what their crown jewels are. If you're a bank, one of your crown jewels should be onboarding customers quickly, easily, and in compliance with regulations. You should reuse this onboarding capability across as many of your products, channels, and customers as possible. This journey typically involves replatforming—moving from silos and spaghetti to reusable digital services organized by platforms, an important feature of a future-ready firm.

3-1 Future-Ready Platform Design Principles

Delight customers through ecosystem integration.

Reduce the channel complexity with compliance built in.

Create a shared data layer for internal and partner use.

Leverage Platform as a Service (PaaS).

Develop plug-and-play core services.

Embed compliance in products/APIs.

Host in the cloud for flexibility.

Source: Michael Harte, MIT CISR industry research fellow.

In a recent research project on replatforming the enterprise, we collaborated with Michael Harte, former chief information officer and chief operating officer of Santander UK, Barclays, and Commonwealth Bank of Australia, and Peter Reynolds, former chief information officer of corporate services and global payments at ANZ Bank and current executive vice president of real time payments at Mastercard, to identify what a future-ready platform would look like (see figure 3-1). A future-ready platform conceptually has six layers with customers at the top connecting through channels, processes, experiences, data, product integration, and infrastructure. Compliance is embedded into both business processes and the products rather than being an afterthought or an add-on. Application programming interfaces (APIs) (or similar) enable plug-and-play modularity. Future-ready platforms help bust a number of myths that many organizations assumed when building previous versions of platforms. For example, a design premise of many platforms in the past—and not true today—was that there was no need to externally share customer data or processes. The size, number, and capabilities of the platforms that a firm needs depend on a firm's situation. The platforms are typically built in stages.

The first phase of pathway 1, building platform capabilities, we call "digitization desert" because to the rest of the firm, it feels like there is no immediate improvement or innovations to show for all the work and investment in digitization. It takes time to simplify the current product offerings, rationalize the business processes, and replatform—often years. The good news is that the new technologies, like cloud computing, microservices, APIs, platforms as a service, and AI, are speeding up the time spent in the digitization desert.

Despite the new approaches, leaders of a pathway 1 transformation—often the CIO or COO—ask line-of-business colleagues to stop (or at least slow down) requesting new systems and wait until the early stages of industrialization are completed, and the digital processes are ready to use and reuse. Of course, line-of-business leaders don't want to wait, and if they have budget and decision rights, they can create local solutions. This is where firms on pathway 1 often fail. Instead of clearly communicating what it will take for all parties in the firm to make progress to the exciting, innovative part of pathway 1, efforts fragment and tensions mount. Line-of-business leaders create a myriad of local solutions making new offers for customers while, at the same time, leaders of operational transformation continue to simplify and rationalize. One good solution to this tense situation is to allocate part of the transformation budget, say 20 percent, to innovative initiatives to delight customers on the condition that the initiatives will be developed as components for later stages of pathway 1. This multiple pathway approach needs to be well-coordinated but is a practical way to both complete the pathway 1 industrialization journey while still improving customer experience and remaining competitive.

Once the build phase successfully creates reusable digital services, firms move into the exploitation phase of rapid innovation. Platforms not only digitize operations to repeatedly execute business processes, but they also provide the information to identify where future profitable growth will come from. Then, with marginal investment, these firms innovate, creating new products that are faster to market because they reuse the platform. Exploitation typically employs new ways of working, like agile teams innovating in short sprints, using and reusing the newly formed services, test-and-learn approaches, minimal viable product creation, and evidence-based decision-making. Exploitation not only improves the way current products are delivered but also creates new and exciting customer offerings generating value for customers and for the firm. Innovation is much faster, as anyone can reuse the data and the modular components created in the first phase.

Firms on pathway 1 create value from operations early as they focus on building their platform capabilities and then work on capturing value from customers and ecosystems as they move through their transformation. This is another good reason to devote, say, 20 percent of your transformation budget to getting to know your customers and developing innovative offerings with digital partners.

On average, the firms that are more than 50 percent complete on pathway 1 have among the best financial performance on both growth and margin relative to competitors, only outperformed by firms on pathway 4. The difference in financial performance between pathway 1 and pathways 2 and 3 is not huge but is statistically significant.

Progressing on Pathway 1:
Kaiser Permanente and Tetra Pak

Traveling along pathway 1 first requires clear goals and a relentless focus on product rationalization, simplification, automation, compliance, and extracting data from processes while creating platforms. The second phase requires rethinking innovation to create new value by reusing the digitized platform services created in new ways. Both phases require organizational changes.

Let's now look at two companies that have made great progress toward becoming future ready following pathway 1. For Kaiser Permanente, a large health system, we will describe how they created a platform mindset in phase one and are now building on this foundation with a new organization focused on creating value from digital. For Tetra Pak, a large manufacturer of food and beverage packaging, we will focus on how they progressed up pathway 1 and managed each of the four explosions, creating value.

Kaiser Permanente: Building a Digital-First Health System

Kaiser Permanente is a leading not-for-profit, integrated health system with 12.5 million members and over 200,000 employees, including more than 85,000 clinicians, and a 2021 operating revenue of $93.1 billion.[6] Their philosophy is to take care of their members holistically and keep them healthy. In the building platform capabilities phase, Kaiser Permanente responded to the disruptive changes in healthcare by developing a "digitally enabled" health system with a direct-to-consumer business model and clinical and business processes enabled with powerful, user-friendly technologies.[7] The organization laid the foundation for its platform mindset transformation in 2004 when it began the rollout of an integrated electronic health record system across all its regions.

Prat Vemana, chief digital officer at Kaiser Permanente, explained:

> *We made the commitment to electronic medical records as our foundation for all of our future transformational work. It did not just capture and store records, but it became the way physicians and clinical staff collaborate to deliver care. It made our organization more powerful as an integrated model of care. It was a big step, and one of the first of such systems in the market.[8]*

Over time, leaders recognized that growing numbers of members were accessing their records on mobile devices, motivating Kaiser Permanente to create a mobile strategy in 2010. The mobile strategy evolved into a holistic consumer digital strategy that the organization considered critical for attracting and retaining members. Diane Comer, chief information and technology officer, explained:

> *Kaiser Permanente's integration of care and coverage is a powerful and distinctive model within the health care industry. This model focuses on delivering high quality, affordable care rather than the common fee-for-service model used elsewhere. The broad array of capabilities underlying the "care and coverage" model spans all aspects of payer and provider offerings and is instantiated in our technology. Our shift to be a digital-first system,*

*coupled with support for physical access for those who
need or want it, has resulted in seamless delivery of
everything from enrollment, to appointment and advice,
to medical records, to prescriptions, to lab work. Our
members and patients have an amazing breadth and
depth of technology available to them via our digital
assets.*[9]

To drive member engagement, the consumer digital strategy focused
on providing personalized and contextually relevant experiences
throughout the process of identifying health issues and selecting
the appropriate channel of interacting with physicians, whether it
be email, phone, video, or in-person visit. As part of the strategy,
Kaiser Permanente carefully weighed digital innovations and
customer expectations regarding privacy.

To leverage the powerful platform, Kaiser Permanente established new ways of working, including a transformation of the IT
organization in 2016 to support the rapid delivery of digital capabilities through DevOps.

In the rapid innovation phase of a pathway 1 transformation,
Kaiser Permanente is transitioning from a "digitally enabled health
system" to a "digital first health system," in Prat Vemana's words.
Kaiser Permanente increasingly leverages digital technologies for
continuous monitoring and intervention. For example, Kaiser
Permanente innovated to solve a big problem with their virtual
cardiac rehabilitation program. There are around 735,000 heart
attacks per year in the United States,[10] and the completion rate of
traditional cardiac rehab programs is only around 50 percent,[11]
leaving many patients vulnerable to setbacks. The healthcare
provider partnered with Samsung in 2018 to develop an at-home program that uses digital technologies (Samsung's wearable devices,

the customized HeartWise app, and Kaiser Permanente's real-time clinical dashboard) to guide rehabilitation after a heart attack.

The innovation team, led by chief innovation and transformation officer Dr. Tadashi Funahashi and Dr. Columbus Batiste (at the time division chief of cardiology and, since 2018, the medical director of the home-based cardiac rehab program) first addressed decision rights—they got clinical, medical, and technology leadership buy-in from the Southern California region and are now expanding to all regions. Then they used a test-and-learn approach to codevelop the program with partner Samsung.[12] They created a small, multidisciplinary core team with people from operations, medical services, technology, and administration. The team collaborated with Samsung partner teams in technology design, user research, engineering, and service development, using human-centered design methods to understand the needs of patients and caregivers. The team developed a prototype, piloted the full app with all rehab components (including exercise, medication, adherence, education, and behavioral modification) with thirty-seven patients over a six-month period, and then provided training and support for regional deployment. Throughout the process, the team measured value in multiple ways, including the bond between patient and provider, via direct patient feedback to doctors, adherence rates, and chart reviews.

In phase one of this pathway 1 transformation, Kaiser Permanente focused on building platform capabilities and creating value from operations and customers. Members who engaged online were healthier and more satisfied, based on Kaiser Permanente's studies. Most importantly, members were twice as likely to stay with Kaiser Permanente if they engaged online.[13]

In the rapid innovation phase, Kaiser Permanente is creating increased value from ecosystem partnerships with innovative digital offerings. For example, customer engagement increased dramatically with the virtual cardiac rehab program. More than 80 percent of patients completed this rehab compared to only 50 percent of patients in-clinic. Operational costs decreased because hospital readmissions were less than 2 percent compared to 10–15 percent for in-clinic programs.[14] "We are taking an existing service, but we are digitally enhancing it in a way that it not only improves the lives of the patient, but also provides efficiencies in the health system," explained Prat Vemana.[15] The longer-term goal is to become a single destination for Kaiser Permanente members, enabling them to manage their health, wellness, and lifestyle holistically around health conditions.

Hiring Kaiser Permanente's first chief digital officer marked the launch of phase two in the transformation in 2019. One of his first steps was to create a new organization, KP Digital, that combined the formerly separate Digital Experience Center (the business side of digital) and the IT group (the technology side of digital). The new Value Management and Data Analysis group was tasked with developing a dashboard that would show where value was being created and help accelerate the spread of ideas and discourage others that were not working. The group characterized value in four areas—membership, utilization, affordability, and quality—and created metrics across four levels, including a CEO dashboard that the executive team and the board review each quarter. In addition, they created a dashboard for experience teams who deliver the digital offerings, which the teams review weekly. These metrics show, for example, how members use new services, like online mailed prescription refills. Because Kaiser

Permanente is in the middle of phase two, most metrics in the value dashboard illuminate value from customers (e.g., number of members) and value to customers. The latter metrics deeply focus on understanding customers and the customer experience across the continuum of care, which includes shopping for coverage, enrolling, managing a health condition (like ordering refills online or signing up for notifications), and many others. One category, named next-level dimension metrics, is about identifying members with unmet needs, medical or social (e.g., food and home security, childcare, literacy), that the health system could address through collaborating with other ecosystem partners like community organizations. The value dashboard is becoming an important tool to measure progress in the rapid innovation phase of pathway 1 by enabling evidence-based decisions.

Tetra Pak: Developing Industry 4.0 and Moving to One Firm for Customer Experience

Tetra Pak, part of the privately owned Tetra Laval Group, is a global market leader in aseptic food and beverage carton packaging, with a total 2020 net sales of €11 billion. While packaging is its biggest source of revenue—the firm produces over 183 billion packages a year—it also offers food processing and adjacent services. Tetra Pak has made significant progress in transformation, primarily following pathway 1, achieving better customer experience through operational excellence, elegantly dealing with the four explosions described in chapter 2.[16] Like Kaiser Permanente, Tetra Pak illustrates a typical order of importance of managing the explosions for pathway 1 firms: (1) changing decision rights; (2) creating a platform mindset; (3) organizational surgery; and (4) new ways of working.

At the start of the twenty-first century, Tetra Pak recognized the importance of operational efficiency on a global scale. Rather than operating as a collective of over 160 firms selling the same base product, management focused on developing a coherent operating model driven by process automation and a single standardized enterprise resource planning solution to become a global firm selling in over 160 countries. Then, in 2015, its strategy and IT departments recognized the potential impact of digital technologies that had become readily available, such as social media, mobile, analytics, cloud, and Internet of Things (IoT) solutions.

Dennis Jönsson, former chief executive officer, explains:

> *Our starting point is strong. We already have a range of industry-leading activities underway in the digital arena; we have put in place a single shared platform on which we run our entire global business; and we have lean and modern IT operations in many areas that provide a solid foundation on which to use information as a strategic asset.*

Tetra Pak's digital transformation effort in the building platform capabilities phase focused on industry 4.0, creating fully integrated collaborative systems that are more efficient and respond in real time to changing customer demands and conditions in factories. The development of a unified plant management service that offers end-to-end control of operations required Tetra Pak to take its platform mindset to the next level. To handle this organizational explosion, Tetra Pak partnered with leading technology firms to help service-enable what made the firm great—its plant operations—and guide the firm on how it could best use its data as a strategic asset. The platform focused on three main areas:

(1) connecting equipment and devices for the provision of useful data across the firm's entire ecosystem; (2) leveraging that data through advanced analytics to conduct predictive maintenance; and (3) making the firm's collective knowledge and expertise available to employees globally through mobile devices and augmented reality. The technology providers were more than suppliers—they understood Tetra Pak's business and engaged in mutual learning. These strategic partnerships were key in ensuring that the firm could experiment and execute its digital strategy on a global scale. This set of activities focused on capturing value from operations.

Unfortunately, the platform did not address the customer experience. Customers still had to deal with representatives from various processing, packaging, and/or services units: "We can say we are one firm all we want, but if we don't change the way we meet the customer, it'll never happen," explained Mark Meyer, chief information officer.

To improve its platform and further differentiate customer offerings in a competitive market, Tetra Pak steadily shifted its focus from operational efficiency toward customer experience, transitioning into the rapid innovation phase. This shift required two additional organizational explosions: a radical change in decision rights triggered the need for organizational surgery. Rather than create a centralized customer experience division, Tetra Pak realigned decision rights with front-end units to improve customer journeys across all touchpoints. Cross-functional key account teams took end-to-end responsibility for customers locally, leveraging a deep understanding of individual customer needs to integrate interactions. This required changes to metrics and incentives, away from back-end efficiencies and cost savings (which became the responsibility of centralized operational divisions) toward sales and net-promoter scores. Although this approach helped solve some initial customer frustrations of dealing with multiple business units, it did not address the underlying business complexity and suboptimization. The packaging, processing, and services silos still existed, and key account managers had limited control over back-end operations—a requirement for further improvement of the customer experience. That is why the firm pursued a major reorganization under the theme "one firm, three businesses"—focusing on what is required to succeed as one firm and how it approaches customers. This set of activities focused on capturing value from customers.

Alongside the other organizational explosions, Tetra Pak is making steady progress toward new ways of working with a large training program to raise awareness and understanding of key elements of the transformation, including industry 4.0 components, customer journey mapping, and the agile methodology. The latter was especially challenging for a firm that has long focused on efficiency and unified operations, as employees were less inclined to use test-and-learn approaches: "[One of the] biggest challenges we're having is the change management with people. I'm not at all worried about the technology. It will work well. It is to change the way people work. That is going to be tremendously difficult," said Goren Liden, IT director.

Today, Tetra Pak focuses on the rapid innovation phase of pathway 1. There are a number of exciting initiatives underway that help Tetra Pak create value from ecosystems. For example, in 2019, Tetra Pak began working on the digitization of food manufacturing in an initiative named "Factory of the Future," with partners, including Microsoft, ABB, SAP, and the automated logistics solutions provider Elettric80.[17] In 2019, Tetra Pak also launched its connected packaging platform to provide end-to-end traceability for producers, greater supply chain visibility for retailers, and more information for customers (including where the product was made, which farm the ingredients came from, and how to recycle the container).[18] In 2020, Tetra Pak developed a new collaborative innovation model to solve some grand challenges. For example, Tetra Pak works with researchers, startups, suppliers (e.g., paperboard manufacturers), and customers (food and beverage brands) on developing packaging solutions with low impact on the environment. The goal was to design a total production plant that would make it easy to simulate, evaluate, and select optimal solutions for specific customers' needs.[19] Laurence Mott, executive vice president of development and engineering, explained:

> *The old notion of a linear supply chain is gone. We need to work in an ecosystem, in close partnerships with our development partners, who also are our suppliers. And at the same time, we need to work in close collaboration with our customers. It's a very, very big challenge to do it all simultaneously.*

Like many firms looking to grow in the digital era, Tetra Pak recognized that it couldn't do it all alone. Digital partnerships will help all parties grew faster.[20] This set of activities focused on capturing value from ecosystems while still building value from customers and operations. Figure 3-2 summarizes how the four explosions were handled at Tetra Pak. We suggest you create a similar diagram for how you will manage explosions in your firm. And then assess how effectively you are managing those explosions!

3-2 How Tetra Pak Dealt with Explosions

Decision Rights

- Transferred efficiency and cost savings efforts from country-specific managing directors to shared services functions
- Realigned responsibilities of country-specific managing directors, assigning them ownership of customer experience, focused on metrics such as sales and NPS
- Restructured performance metrics and incentives with a focus on sales and customer journeys (rather than efficiency)

New Ways of Working

- Created training programs on digitalization and Industry 4.0 to raise awareness and understanding of the potential of disruptive technologies for the organization
- Introduced agile methodologies (where applicable) in product development and IT

Platform Mindset

- Developed a single-plant management service that offered end-to-end plant control
- Partnered with technology leaders to secure the best possible Industry 4.0 solutions for the connected workforce, advanced analytics, and connected solutions

Organizational Surgery

- Took an existing centralization effort to the next level—"one company, three businesses"

Source: Interviews with company executives; company documents.

What Leaders Should Focus On

The most important leadership task for successfully traveling along pathway 1 to future ready is clearly describing the pathway you are on to your people—over and over again. Employees really need to understand that there are two distinct phases in pathway 1: building platforms and then rapid innovation. Each phase has a different focus for value creation and explosions (see figure 3-3).

3-3 Pathway 1—What Leaders Should Focus On

Explosion	Value
Decision Rights	Operations
Platform Mindset	Customers
New Ways of Working	Ecosystems
Organizational Surgery	

Future Ready

Build platforms

Silos and Spaghetti

Rapidly innovate

Source: The posited order of the actions results from our qualitative research. We tested our hypothesis that decision rights was the explosion to anticipate and manage first using hierarchical regression equations and the data from the MIT CISR 2019 Top Management Teams and Transformation Survey (N = 1,311).

Building Platforms

The building platforms phase requires firms to identify their crown jewels and then build digitized platforms to turn them into reusable digital services. The building of these platforms takes time, often more than a year, and leaders need to help everyone understand why this build time is important and what to expect and when. The largest value, and therefore focus, in this first phase comes from operations, but firms also create some value from customers and from ecosystems (which increase in the rapid innovation phase). Measuring that value, sharing success stories, and explaining how these platforms create the foundation for future success is a critical part of the leadership role for pathway 1.

Creating a platform mindset is critical to the success of this phase. For some firms, this platform mindset is quite natural—manufacturing firms often find creating a platform mindset around digital a natural extension of what they have done on the shop floor and in supply chains. But for other firms (e.g., many banks, insurance companies, professional services, and educational institutions), it is culturally a big change to move from creating local solutions to creating reusable platforms. Changing decision rights has to be tackled first, particularly in firms that are used to creating local solutions.

To effectively navigate the digitization desert at the beginning of pathway 1, senior leadership has to shift the decision rights balance away from the product and customer experience people to the operations leaders and platform builders. For example, there will be a lot of demand for new features to better serve customers to be added to the platforms that are under construction. Who gets to decide whether these new features are added and when? For firms that manage the digitization desert successfully, decisions are typically made jointly by operations and customer experience leaders but weighted perhaps slightly in favor of operations so they can take responsibility for building and delivering the platforms. This is not an easy political challenge to manage, and it requires transparency and good metrics. As you think about how you will do this in your firm, we suggest you review how Tetra Pak manages the explosions (see figure 3-2).

Rapid Innovation

The earlier you can begin the rapid innovation phase, the better—reducing the time in the digitization desert! One of the leadership lessons from pathway 1 is to build the platforms so that the digital services come online in phases and can be used for innovation rather than waiting for the platform to be completed. For example, if you're building a mortgage platform for a bank, and two of the services required are "customer onboarding" and "customer identity," those services can be used before the full mortgage offering is complete.

Value from operations continues to accrue in the rapid innovation phase, but value from customers and ecosystems increases more rapidly and therefore requires more attention from leaders. Adding metrics for value from customers and ecosystems at this stage is important. This mindset change typically requires focus on the last two explosions—new ways of working and organizational surgery.

New ways of working, like test-and-learn approaches and evidence-based decision-making, help speed up innovation. Like Amazon and other platform companies, you can now test several different strategies with your customers and get feedback very quickly through A/B testing.

These new ways of working and other changes typically surface a need for organizational surgery. The surgery is often around reorganizing to bring the customer-facing skills together with the operational data and digital skills to facilitate that rapid innovation. We have not observed any one best way to do this, but often it's about creating more horizontal capabilities—for example, shared services or reusable modules that the customer-facing verticals can use to rapidly innovate.

In chapter 7, we will introduce a dashboard to help you create, measure, and capture the value from operations, customers, and ecosystems with two lenses (i.e., what value is created and how the value was created through capabilities). As you lead a pathway 1 transformation, we ask you to prepare by identifying your key metrics for each of these three types of value and the capabilities you plan to develop to drive them.

Action Items from Chapter 3

The first three actions are common to every transformation.

1. Communicate today (and every day) that your firm is focusing on a pathway 1 transformation to become future ready. Paint a picture of what working in the firm will look like in the future, and articulate the steps along the way to help people understand their roles.

2. Collect stories of early success and distribute them widely—internally and externally. It's those early indicators of success that help keep motivation high, drive commitment and progress, and stem the impact of the doubters.

3. Create a plan for managing the explosions.

4. As part of your firm's communication plan about proceeding on pathway 1, describe the two phases in pathway 1—building platforms and exploiting those platforms to rapidly innovate—each with a different focus, actions, and value creation. The building platforms phase requires firms to identify their crown jewels and then build digitized platforms to turn those jewels into reusable digital services. The rapidly innovating phase typically requires that the firm implement new ways of working and focus on reusing the capabilities from the build phase. Elaborate with details what will happen at each phase in your firm.

5. Try to begin the rapid innovation phase as soon as possible, ideally well before ending the building platforms

phase. This will reduce the time your firm spends in the digitization desert and speed up value creation.

6. Identify and track metrics of operational value.

7. Review the Kaiser Permanente and Tetra Pak examples to identify good ideas that can be adjusted to align with your firm's culture.

Chapter 4

Pathway 2

Delight Customers First

Pathway 2 is about delighting customers. Multidisciplinary teams from all over the firm innovate using digital technologies, better data, and new ways of working to engage and delight customers. For most firms, it works brilliantly, and almost everybody is happier. Customers love the new services and respond with higher customer experience scores. It is not unusual for the net-promoter score (NPS) to go up twenty points or more and revenue growth to follow. Firms that have moved up into the integrated experience quadrant had revenue growth that was 9.6 percentage points higher (relative to their industry average) compared to firms in the silos and spaghetti quadrant—a massive premium.[1]

The multidisciplinary teams work and innovate in new ways and make their customers happy by creating new offerings. But all of this local innovation doesn't address the underlying complexity of the product offerings and systems, and this usually makes it worse, driving up the cost to serve the customer. Also, pathway 2 is hard, in the beginning, on other parts of the enterprise. For instance, customer service people often struggle because they are responsible for integrating a customer's experience across multiple offerings (and channels and systems) as, typically, the multidisciplinary teams creating the local innovations do not deal with that challenge. Therefore, the customer service people jump between systems, memorizing data and codes to smooth over the silos and spaghetti to provide a better experience for the customer. It is also typically hard on the IT group that integrates and secures these new offerings—or at least makes them compatible. And finance finds this part of a pathway 2 transformation challenging because they should measure the cost to serve, which is not often done.

At some point, the senior executives change the focus of the transformation initiatives to increasing operational efficiency, moving the organization to the right on our framework. This part of the journey is typically easier than the digitization desert on pathway 1 because of the success already achieved in delighting customers.

Why Follow Pathway 2 and What to Expect

Around 18 percent of all firms in our latest survey primarily adopt pathway 2 for their transformations.[2] These firms typically have a desire or need to dramatically increase their customers' experience but don't have time to build the new firm-wide digital service capabilities by following pathway 1. The need is often driven by a perception that a large percent of firm revenues is under threat from digital disruption over the next five years. Firms following pathway 2 estimate that 39 percent of their revenues will be lost in five years if they don't change, compared to only 26 percent for firms following pathway 1. The combination of a relatively poor current customer experience and/or a higher perceived level of threat is the key driver for taking this path. On average, the firms that complete more than half of pathway 2 have very good financial performance on both growth and margin relative to competitors. They perform almost on par with pathway 1 and pathway 4 firms and above pathway 3.

Pathway 2 has two phases: first, the customer delight phase and then the consolidation and replatform phase. The first phase is the strategic response to the firm's competitive position in the marketplace. For example, if you are a retail clothing firm with a large store footprint that pivoted to online sales during the Covid-19 pandemic, you'll likely need to improve your omnichannel customer experience, and pathway 2 makes great sense. You may open online stores in new markets with no or very few physical stores, as we saw many brands do. By first delighting customers and then consolidating, simplifying, and creating a base of reusable components (typically on new platforms), the firm moves to become future ready.

There are some interesting industry differences among firms picking pathway 2. For example, 29 percent of consumer, 25 percent of banking, and 22 percent of insurance firms pick pathway 2—well above the average of 18 percent. In contrast, only 9 percent of heavy industry, 6 percent of services, 11 percent of manufacturing, and 4 percent of healthcare organizations pick pathway 2.

The first phase of pathway 2 focuses on delighting customers by finding ways to amplify the customer's voice inside the firm and developing better offers for them. Delighting customers often requires a change of firm mindset from "inside out" to "outside in." To achieve the outside-in perspective, many firms focus on their customers' journeys to better understand when to engage with customers, where there is friction in the interaction, and how to delight them. They find their customer journeys often occur across multiple channels and involve multiple products, requiring significantly more integration of the organizational silos than before. A fast and practical way to help integrate those silos is to create multidisciplinary teams that represent the silos at the point of contact to the customer.

One of the challenges of following pathway 2 is that many different parts of the business with customer-facing responsibilities all feel empowered to focus on local innovations that create better (local) customer experiences. This is a heady time of creativity and offering new value to customers. The process is addictive because, for most firms, focusing on customer experience works well, resulting in rising NPS and increasing revenues. Firms accumulate and track value from customers. Many create some value from ecosystems early by including selected digital offerings by partners in their channels. The instinct is to do more of what's been working and invest in further local innovations. And this next round of innovations could also work well, leading to further increases in customer experience and revenue.

But there is also evidence of diminishing returns as this innovation process continues if the firm does not begin to shift the focus of its digital initiatives to create value from operations. The firm won't get quite as good a return on the fourth round of innovation as the first. This occurs because it adds more layers of systems, particularly local systems, on top of the already complex landscape of processes and technology, thus increasing costs and slowing down the response times. Worse still, pathway 2 has the lowest employee experience of the four pathways because you are increasing the cognitive load on the employees as they jump from one system to another to meet the needs of the customer.[3] And there is an avalanche of new offerings that customer experience people have to learn and integrate with the ones they already know. Pathway 2 sees the highest rate of frustration and burnout among customer experience employees.

At this point, the financial folks often start to see reductions in margin even though revenue increases. Most firms don't accurately measure the cost to serve customers, but if they did, they would see it going up as the firm moves along pathway 2. This pathway is a great choice for firms that need to dramatically increase their customer experience. At the same time, however, they should start to measure the cost to serve so that they know when to change direction and focus on consolidating new systems and replatforming. If the finance teams don't measure the cost to serve, there is often no driving force to slow down local innovation and focus on creating value from operations.

The consolidate and replatform phase of pathway 2 is similar to the digitization desert phase of pathway 1, but the destination is clearer, and it is easier to manage expectations as successes from digital are already evident. The consolidate and replatform phase can also more specifically target the digital services the firm already knows are needed. The delight-the-customer phase is effectively a series of experiments to determine what services are needed, which can then be created at scale in the consolidate and replatform phase. The downside of a successful delight-the-customer phase in pathway 2 is that the increased complexity from the local experiments must also be unraveled and integrated—alongside the already existing silos and spaghetti—in the consolidate and replatform phase.

Progressing on Pathway 2: CarMax and CEMEX

Let's now take a look at two firms that pursued a digital transformation on pathway 2. CarMax illustrates how an already successful firm operating in the physical world establishes new ways of working to create a successful new omnichannel business model. CEMEX operates in the physical world but focuses its digital transformation on delivering a superior customer experience with digital engagement.

CarMax: Creating a Seamless Omnichannel Experience

When CarMax began operating in the 1990s, they realized that the car buying and selling experience was fragmented and difficult. The goal of CarMax, from the early years, was to treat people with respect and operate with transparency, thus improving the customer experience.[4] The firm described its purpose as follows: "At CarMax, our commitment to innovation and iconic customer experiences have made us the nation's largest retailer of used cars. As the original disruptor of the automotive industry, our 'no-haggle' prices transformed car buying and selling from a stressful, dreaded event into the honest, straightforward experience all people deserve."[5] In recent years, CarMax reinvented itself to become an omnichannel business with a pathway 2 transformation. The vision for the recent transformation was to engage customers wherever and whenever they wanted. In August 2020, CarMax made significant progress in phase two (consolidate and replatform) with the rollout of their omnichannel platform.[6] Growth was spectacular, with CarMax opening more than two hundred thirty stores in forty-one states and becoming the largest seller and buyer of used automobiles to and from customers in the United States, with revenues over $31.9 billion in fiscal year 2022. CarMax also has a long-standing reputation for being a great place to work and applying technology to make it easier for associates to provide a great customer experience.[7] For example, CarMax introduced a QR code window sticker so that the status (and details) of each car was quickly identifiable, connecting the physical and the digital worlds and making the associates' jobs easier. In 2021, CarMax introduced another innovation—the online Instant Offer Appraisal tool—which enabled customers selling their cars to receive an offer from CarMax in less than two minutes. Like in-store appraisals, offers were free, valid for seven days, and independent of the purchase of a new car. CarMax EVP and chief information and technology officer Shamim Mohammad explains: "Instant Offer has been an incredible success. The technology behind it makes it really easy for consumers to use, and the response has been amazing. Since we launched the product in early 2021, we've bought more than 707,000 cars through the tool, representing over half of our total buys of vehicles during that time."[8]

There were many aspects to the success of CarMax's transformation to an omnichannel business, but we will highlight two key explosions. First, establishing new ways of working by creating cross-functional teams that use test-and-learn methods (important for phase one). Second, supporting the platform mindset by building dashboards to measure progress on value from customers, ecosystems, and operations for all to see (important for phase two). Please see the case study by our MIT CISR colleagues Jeanne Ross, Cynthia Beath, and Ryan Nelson for the full story.[9]

New Ways of Working with Cross-Functional Teams

To reinvent the customer experience to become truly omnichannel, CarMax stood up customer-facing product teams in five areas across the customer journey: acquiring, transporting, merchandising, selling, and financing vehicles. The goal of each multidisciplinary team was to work independently to create elements of a great customer experience using digital platforms and data. Jim Lyski, chief marketing officer, explains how the teams were organized:

> *What we start with is what we consider a bite-sized piece of the customer experience. So, we may say digital merchandising is a bite. How do we immerse the consumer into the vehicle online? And as we go, if it's a little too big, we break it up, and it becomes two teams with two missions.*[10]

Teams set their goals using OKRs (objectives and key results), ran two-week sprints to deliver on their OKRs, and reported progress in biweekly meetings called open houses. The open houses not only served as a forum for teams to share what they had done and get input from others but also to coordinate the teams to better meet CarMax's overall goals.

Each team was focused on identifying new opportunities and new ways to work. Once a great new idea was identified, the focus shifted to scaling to monetize the innovation. Shamim Mohammad reflects on the power of their multidisciplinary teams. "Empower the teams, give them the goal, tell them what you want to achieve. Then stand back while they figure out how, and do all these experiments. They will exceed your expectations, repeatedly."[11]

Platform Mindset with Dashboards

CarMax created dashboards to make performance transparent and connect teams in real time. As teams worked feverishly in their two-week sprints to meet their OKRs, they could connect their efforts to the bigger picture of value from customers. Gautam Puranick, chief data officer and head of business strategy and analytics, explains:

> *We have a daily dashboard that shows the number of web visits, how many people hit our website and our apps yesterday, how many people took the next step of saying, "Hey, I'm interested in a car," which is what we call a lead. . . . So, every day, all these teams are focused on their piece of the pie. And that's sort of the marriage of micro and macro.*[12]

The omnichannel transformation positioned the firm for growth in retail, wholesale, and auto finance. CarMax was expanding into the broader used auto ecosystem. To track the omnichannel performance, CarMax introduced new key performance indicators to track progress on value, including value from operations, both quarterly and annually:[13]

- Percent of used units sold online

- Percent of revenue from online transactions

- Online appraisal buys (CarMax online car purchases based on instant appraisals)

- Cost: selling, general & administrative expenses (SG&A) as a percentage of gross profit

Pathway 2 is all about delighting customers in new ways. The new digital tools, particularly platforms, data, and analytics, coupled with the new ways of working—like test-and-learn approaches by multidisciplinary teams working in short sprints—enable exciting possibilities. For another example, we'll look at the construction industry—a complex, fragmented, cyclical industry not known for its great customer experience. It is in these types of industries that we are seeing some of the biggest improvements in customer experience by adopting pathway 2 approaches.

CEMEX: Delivering a Superior Customer Experience with CEMEX Go

CEMEX is a building materials firm headquartered in Monterrey, Mexico. CEMEX is focused on four core businesses—cement, ready-mix concrete, aggregates, and urbanization solutions in over fifty countries.[14] CEMEX operates in the highly fragmented construction industry that has been reliant on personal relationships, paperwork, and traditional ways of doing business—often resulting in an uneven customer experience and inefficiencies. The construction industry, like many fragmented industries, was ripe for transformation. Fernando A. González, chief executive officer of CEMEX, summarizes the opportunity: "The future for our industry will be driven by the quality of the customer experience, not just the quality of the products and services. Our customers are increasingly expecting to have the same kind of experiences in working with businesses that they have in the consumer space."[15]

CEMEX spent considerable time in the early 2000s improving its operations to gain global efficiencies through process standardization (called the CEMEX Way) and building a strong reputation for quality, safety, and materials innovation. The focus on delivering a superior customer experience enabled by digital technologies was a new frontier for achieving the firm's purpose of providing resilient infrastructure and energy efficient building solutions. Starting in 2014, the top management team initiated a new digital transformation they designed in two phases.

First Phase: Focus on Customer Experience

In the first phase, CEMEX focused on developing new capabilities for customer experience by creating a digital channel and then extending it to an omnichannel experience. González wanted customers to be able to complete the full journey on one digital platform. He also wanted the experience to be seamless, no matter if a customer started the journey and placed an order on or off the digital platform.

The breakthrough initiative was CEMEX Go, launched in November 2017 with deployment completed in early 2019. The CEMEX Go online store offered the full digital customer journey—discovering CEMEX, becoming a customer, placing an order, receiving products, receiving invoices, and receiving support. For example, the job of the construction site manager, a key customer persona, was very challenging. Managers made many decisions each day with little information and often didn't know when ordered items would arrive or what delays would occur. To deliver on the promise of a superior customer experience enabled by digital technologies, CEMEX focused on putting everything construction site managers needed in one place—on their mobile devices.

To enable the new digital and omnichannel customer experience, an important part of the first phase was integrating CEMEX Go with a new order fulfillment system and a new customer relationship management system to replace the traditional manually assisted back-end processes behind the customer interface. The integration enabled the new digital confirmation capability, an automatic review of inventory, transport, and other components of the customer journey when an order is confirmed online.

By 2020, the results of the first transformation phase were excellent, with an NPS score of 67, an increase from 50 in 2019 and 44 in 2018.[16] Fifty-two percent of global sales were processed through CEMEX Go, and about 90 percent of recurring customers used the service.[17] During the Covid-19 pandemic, CEMEX Go allowed customers to work seamlessly in a low-touch environment. CEMEX licenses the CEMEX Go platform to other firms in the construction industry, creating value from ecosystems.[18]

Second Phase: Focus on Cost-to-Serve

In the second phase, CEMEX is focusing on operational efficiency and reducing cost-to-serve while continuing to improve customer experience.

Further automation of the order fulfillment processes is helping reduce cost-to-serve. By 2022, CEMEX had automated order fulfillment for cement (a product type). But automating the process for ready-mix concrete (another product type) was more complex. CEMEX developed artificial intelligence (AI) and machine learning (ML) capabilities to tackle this problem. They added a new capability—predicting potential cancellations—to the internal ready-mix management system (RMS). The next step is launching a dynamic pricing system for time slots. These new capabilities will be included in CEMEX's automated digital confirmation capability for the ready-mix product type.

In addition to the continuing focus on value from customers and value from operations, CEMEX is placing greater focus on creating new value from ecosystems with digital initiatives that continue the focus on improving customer experience. In the words of Luis Hernandez, executive vice president of digital and organization development, these are some of the most promising ecosystem initiatives coming from the company's digital innovation efforts. For example:

- CEMEX created a company, Arkik, to commercialize the RMS as Software as a Service (SaaS) for independent ready-mix customers who can improve their own operations and connect with CEMEX Go's order fulfillment. The plan is to create a platform for managing and orchestrating products from CEMEX, helping those customers share resources and optimize their networks.

- CEMEX's building materials distribution network, Construrama, is the largest retail building material store in Mexico and in Latin American countries where CEMEX is present. In 2018, CEMEX launched the Construrama Online Store to continue efforts to transform the construction industry. Sergio Menéndez, vice president of distributor sales of CEMEX in Mexico, said, "Our clients will now enjoy easy access to a wider catalog of products and be able to select, purchase, and follow up on their online order, generating significant savings in productivity for our Construrama network of retail stores, builders, and final customers."[19]

- Launched in April 2019, the CEMEX Go Developer Center opened the platform, connecting CEMEX processes with customers via application programming interfaces (APIs) (i.e., customer information, CEMEX Go orders, ticket management, financial documents, construction industry solutions, and CEMEX plants).[20] For example, customers could integrate their enterprise resource planning system with CEMEX Go to order building materials. In a 2019 press release, González explained, "CEMEX Go Developer Center is the natural next step in the successful advancement of our digital platform, after reaching more than 30,000 clients in all of the countries in which we operate. Digital ecosystems are changing the traditional parameters that firms use to compete, and this new stage of CEMEX Go will enable us to maintain our leadership of the digital transformation of the global construction materials industry."[21]

- CEMEX Ventures (the venture capital and open innovation unit of CEMEX, launched in 2017) invested in new value propositions across the construction ecosystem. CEMEX Ventures creates an "open and collaborative platform to lead the revolution of the construction industry . . . and shape tomorrow's value ecosystem."[22] In 2022, CEMEX Ventures collaborated with and invested in twenty startups, focusing on long-term impact on the construction ecosystem. In 2021, CEMEX joined the Open-Built industry initiative to codevelop a platform connecting firms across the global building industry.[23]

Let's now take a look at how CEMEX pursued key explosions. In the first phase, CEMEX focused on creating a process for the digital transformation effort and connecting IT and the business.

This decision by the CEO was the first among several changes in decision rights that directly affected funding and project approvals throughout CEMEX. Although the CEO was fully involved in the digital business transformation effort, he did not lead it alone. First, he delegated responsibility to three separate areas: commercial development, processes and information technology, and human resources. Then, as the transformation grew in importance, he shifted the responsibility to shared ownership by the executive committee. Simultaneously, the executive committee recognized that true customer experience improvements required greater autonomy for digital development teams, along with major changes relating to new ways of working. CEMEX introduced agile methodologies and formed scrum teams to develop platform services. The minimum viable product concept helped them learn and work with other departments—such as operations—as they developed the platform, which is now on iteration 5.0.

Engaging employees in the transformation was critical. CEMEX's new strategic direction and the concepts, practices, and tools needed to implement that strategy were shared widely. Blended learning and development programs (which leveraged face-to-face training with online learning platforms) laid the groundwork for CEMEX's digital business transformation. Particularly important was the development of a "digital mindset," which comprised five components:

1. A focus on customer centricity and customer journeys

2. Iterative (time-boxed) work processes

3. Collaborative work habits that transcend silos and hierarchies

4. Test-and-learn environments that foster experimentation

5. Embracing continuous change

CEMEX recognized that they needed to understand customers better to drive adoption of the platform. While in the past, IT had relied on input from the business managers, they now developed systematic, continuous conversations with customers on all new developments. In a discovery process, employees conducted 172 customer interviews, panel discussions, and customer surveys to map customer journeys and identify customer pain points in dealing with CEMEX. The primary finding was an unmet industry need for real-time information and transparency to improve decision-making, productivity, and operational control. CEMEX employees experimented with new customer-facing initiatives and collaborated with a technology partner to develop new custom applications. Executive education, as well as workshops on topics related to digital business transformation, helped CEMEX's senior leadership team to develop a common language to guide and align the firm's customer-facing efforts toward developing a single platform—CEMEX Go.

New ways of working were followed by developing a platform mindset that focused on simplifying and streamlining customers' interactions with the firm. Customers referred to CEMEX Go as a "one-stop shop," a platform that allowed them to seamlessly place, schedule, or adjust an order; receive instant notifications of their order status; track delivery trucks in real time from the moment they left CEMEX facilities; and manage invoices and payments for those orders from multiple devices (including computers, smartphones, tablets, and smartwatches). CEMEX's commercial network, which represents all business units, created a new organization named Commercial Development that was responsible for customer engagement.

CEMEX was able to quickly develop its customer-facing platform and scale it worldwide, and customers loved it, driving increased value. However, CEMEX soon had to shift its attention and investments back toward operational improvements, starting phase 2 of the digital transformation on pathway 2. "We had to push the brakes. We could not continue evolving without taking care of some bugs and back-end issues that were escalating to a level that was not healthy. If we didn't fix those, the adoption rate would start to decline," said Fausto Sosa, information technology VP.[24] CEMEX added production and management processes to the transformation agenda and created two new platforms to complement CEMEX Go: SmartOps for production and Working Smarter to optimize support management processes (e.g., for record-to-report, procure-to-pay, hire-to-retire).

The global rollout of CEMEX Go required further standardization of many of CEMEX's processes, solutions, and (former) shadow IT efforts. Organizational surgery facilitated this standardization effort. CEMEX split its traditional IT department into a "digital enablement" unit (comprising customer-facing projects, analytics, and the development of CEMEX's digital capabilities/platform) and a "global IT operations" unit (comprising data centers, sourcing/partnerships, and CEMEX's IT operational backbone). These units also introduced new job functions (e.g., advanced global analytics and user experience and design) and new local customer experience offices to consolidate local customer priorities.

In 2019, CEMEX created two new organization areas that report directly to the CEO. The organizational surgery was aimed at breaking down silos further as CEMEX integrated their three platforms—CEMEX Go, SmartOps, and Working Smarter. The areas are (1) sustainability, commercial and operations development, and (2) digital and organization development (DoD). The first area includes commercial development, supply chain management, and operations. The second includes digital enablement, information technology, human resources, CEMEX Ventures, and Neoris (a transformation consulting company owned by CEMEX).[25] CEMEX Ventures was made part of the DoD organization to better connect external market exploration with solutions to address customer needs. The organizational surgery was supported by other initiatives around new ways of working, including a learning program to acquire digital capability at all levels of the firm, starting with ExCo and Country Presidents, and hiring more than one hundred talented graduates of digital native careers to accelerate the digital culture within the organization.

Figure 4-1 highlights how each of the four explosions were managed at CEMEX. CEO Fernando González explained,

> *Deciding which particular pathway to follow was just the first step in our business transformation journey; the bigger challenge as a CEO was to closely manage the organizational changes (or explosions, using MIT CISR's term) required to build a truly digital enterprise. Beyond the technological implications, the change management efforts need to be at the top of the CEO agenda.*[26]

An excellent exercise for the leaders of your transformation is to create a similar diagram to figure 4-1 for your firm on how effectively you are managing your explosions!

4-1 How CEMEX Dealt with Explosions

✣ Decision Rights

- Focused investments on customer experience initiatives, led by a fully involved CEO
- Moved transformation control to executive committee responsibility
- Provided more autonomy to digital development teams

🜨 New Ways of Working

- Leveraged existing discipline in efficient operations and safety on customer-centricity
- Trained organization on creating a digital mindset: more agile, collaborative, iterative, and less hierarchical
- Aligned firm transformation efforts through executive education programs for senior management and management-led workshops

✈ Platform Mindset

- Developed an integrated multidevice digital platform servicing the end-to-end customer journey
- Standardized processes and solutions, eliminating shadow IT efforts
- Explored an open ecosystem using APIs, followed with a successful launch of the CEMEX Go external developer platform

⚕ Organizational Surgery

- Split IT into two units—digital enablement (customer focused) and global IT operations (enterprise focused)
- Created local customer experience offices and new digital-specific functions (e.g., UX/design, digital architecture)
- Stood up two new units—sustainability, commercial, and operations development; and digital and organization development

Source: Interviews with company executives; company documents.

What Leaders Should Focus On

The most important leadership task for successfully traveling along pathway 2 (like for pathway 1) to future ready is clearly describing the pathway you are on to your people and other stakeholders—over and over again. People need to understand that there are two

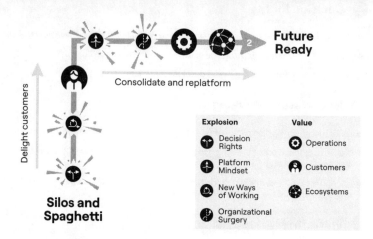

4-2 Pathway 2—What Leaders Should Focus On

Future Ready

Consolidate and replatform

Delight customers

Silos and Spaghetti

Explosion

Decision Rights

Platform Mindset

New Ways of Working

Organizational Surgery

Value

Operations

Customers

Ecosystems

Source: The posited order of the actions results from our qualitative research. We tested our hypothesis that decision rights was the explosion to anticipate and manage first using hierarchical regression equations and the data from the MIT CISR 2019 Top Management Teams and Transformation Survey (N = 1,311).

distinct phases in pathway 2—delighting customers and then consolidating and replatforming. Each phase requires a different focus for value creation and management of organizational explosions (see figure 4-2).

Delighting Customers

The delighting customers phase of pathway 2 is typically full of excitement and enthusiasm by the multidisciplinary teams that are creating new customer offers and revitalizing existing ones to improve the customer experience. The new ways of working that we describe in this chapter are exciting and addictive. Most firms unlock a not-before-seen digital innovation capability that has a big and measurable impact on the customer experience. The resulting increases in net-promoter score or similar measures create great enthusiasm to continue this local innovation.

Early on in this innovation process, it's important to capture and widely share the stories of successes. Employees see this innovation is happening, but it is equally important for customers, investors, and partners to be aware of the process. These early successes typically built on themselves and create even better and bigger ideas going forward as well as more optimism for the future.

Dashboards, or some other way to measure the impact, are important at this stage to share the successes and measure the three types of value: customer, operations, and ecosystems. As figure 4-2 illustrates, the most important value to track first is the value from customers, followed by operations and then ecosystems.

As in all pathways, decision rights is the most important explosion to start with. Typically, this means empowering local teams to create and improve customer offers and removing obstacles, like governance, slow budget processes, and risk, technology, HR, and finance departments dragging their heels requiring approvals or other interventions that slow things down. One bank we worked with was so frustrated with the slowness of the risk group that they added a risk person to each agile team and gave them a risk cap they could approve without going to the centralized risk office—this worked really well.

Soon after decision rights are addressed, firms need to focus on new ways of working. Explicitly managing new ways of working is important for fast-tracking along pathway 2. These new ways of working need training, tools, sharing of experiences, and other interventions to make them happen faster, as we saw in CarMax.

A dashboard is also important to begin identifying needed course corrections if the innovation isn't happening fast enough and then to track the cost to serve. Understanding how quickly the cost to serve is increasing is important in determining when to move to the consolidating and replatforming phase.

Consolidating and Replatforming

The consolidate and replatform phase is very similar to the digitization desert phase of pathway 1 but typically easier given the success achieved so far. The design specification of the needed platforms typically comes out of the first phase as the teams identify what new technology capabilities are needed to further delight customers. This is where the focus on value from operations occurs through the platform mindset explosion. As we saw in CEMEX, this phase is often accompanied by some organizational surgery to better deliver on the new priorities. The consolidate and replatform phase differs from pathway 1 in that customer innovation continues and is iteratively connected to the new platforms. It is this iteration that helps speed the firm toward becoming future ready.

Action Items from Chapter 4

The first three actions are common to every transformation.

1. Communicate today (and every day) that your firm is focusing on a pathway 2 transformation to become future ready. Paint a picture of what working at the firm will look like in the future, and articulate the steps along the way to help people understand their roles.

2. Collect stories of early success and distribute them widely—internally and externally. It's those early indicators

of success that help keep motivation high, drive commitment and progress, and stem the impact of the doubters.

3. Create a plan for managing the explosions.

4. As part of your firm's communication plan about proceeding on pathway 2, describe the two phases—delighting customers and consolidating and replatforming—each with a different focus, actions, and value creation. The delighting customers phase typically involves amplifying the customer's voice inside the organization and using that understanding to create new offers. The consolidating and replatforming phase typically requires firms to identify their crown jewels and then build digitized platforms to turn those into reusable digital services. This phase usually builds on the delighting customers phase and specifically targets the digital services the firm now knows it needs. Elaborate with details on what will happen in each phase at your firm.

5. Ensure you measure the cost-to-serve, usually done by a team in finance, to identify when your firm should move to the consolidate and replatform phase. Identify the group that is going to be your firm's traffic cop.

6. Identify and track metrics about customer value.

7. Review the approaches taken by CarMax and CEMEX to identify good ideas that can be customized to align with your firm's culture.

Chapter 5

Pathway 3

Alternate the Focus, like Stair Steps

This chapter is all about taking a disciplined alternating focus between customer experience and operational efficiency on pathway 3. This pathway is the most popular because it makes perfect sense to many firms to deliver smaller but tangible improvements in customer experience and then operational efficiency and back again, balancing the improvements on each dimension along the way. However, firms that choose pathway 3—which looks like stair steps—have a surprisingly higher risk with a slightly lower-than-average financial performance. The challenge is to synchronize all the different activities. To successfully follow pathway 3, the firm must be disciplined in scoping shorter digital initiatives (e.g., six to twelve months in duration), completing them, and then sustaining the value creation of each initiative on the stair steps so that those benefits can be passed on to the next digital initiative.

In this chapter, we will explore the stair steps of pathway 3 and identify the key practices required for success, particularly around synchronization. We have observed firms as they progress on their pathway 3 transformation eventually, after a lot of practice, smooth out the stair steps to travel a 45° line toward future ready, simultaneously increasing the customer experience and operational efficiency through connected, coordinated digital initiatives.

Why Follow Pathway 3 and What to Expect

Pathway 3 is the most popular, with 26 percent of all firms we studied. Pathway 3 is more evenly distributed across industries than the other pathways. Consumer is the industry most represented by pathway 3, with mining, oil, and gas the least represented.[1] Firms following pathway 3 typically need to improve both their customer experience and operational efficiency at approximately the same time. This need is driven, in part, by a perception that their revenues are under a high level of threat from digital disruption in the next five years. Firms following pathway 3 estimate that 37 percent of their revenues will be lost in five years if they don't change, compared to 26 percent for pathway 1 firms (the lowest) or 39 percent for pathway 2 firms. With similar levels of threat on pathway 2 and pathway 3, firm leaders must think about what is driving that threat, as it impacts the decision of which pathway to follow. If your firm is primarily facing competition around customers, follow pathway 2. If your firm can't untangle whether the threat is primarily external around the expectations of customers or internal because of system complexity and costs, the pathway 3 transformation is likely the best bet. For pathway 3 to succeed, the firm has to identify a set of projects that address the threat and are both connectable and manageable to do in, say, six to twelve months each. Firms following pathway 3 believe that they can make smaller steps of improvement in customer experience and operational efficiency and incrementally reach future ready without multiyear commitments on pathway 1 to efficiency or pathway 2 to customer experience. Most importantly, firms following pathway 3 believe (sometimes naively) that they can synchronize effectively, switching their focus in smaller and, therefore, less risky steps.

Firms on pathway 3 toggle between focusing on digital initiatives that create value from customers and operations. These firms then have the additional job of coordinating to make it all work together to continue capturing both types of value in much shorter iterations than pathways 1 and 2. The first area of focus can be whichever the firm perceives to be the most important at the commencement of the transformation journey. For example, if a financial services firm can't wait to improve customer experience but believes a few initiatives will make a big difference, they can start by building a new banking app. Then, the firm shifts its focus to operational efficiency and might create an application programming interface (API) layer to speed up future innovation. Then, the firm shifts back to a customer focus and builds real-time customized offers using the new APIs. Next, for more operational efficiency, they focus on simplification and moving systems capabilities to the cloud. Synchronization focuses the firm's attention on prioritizing the appropriate steps, creating and capturing value from each step, and leveraging the new capabilities in the next step to steadily progress toward future ready.

Synchronizing is the critical ingredient for success with pathway 3. We found there are four key elements to synchronizing the stair steps of connected digital initiatives (not necessarily in this order):

- **Motivate:** setting a vision for how the firm will transform and show how employees' actions contribute to success

- **Prioritize:** selecting, often from a long wish list, the key digital initiatives along the stair steps that will cumulatively create value

- **Innovate:** increasing the digital innovation of the firm, enabling the key digital initiatives

- **Coordinate:** ensuring that the value created at each step is passed along to the next step through evidence-based decisions, keeping track of progress through dashboarding, and fostering communication

Firms on pathway 3 achieve both value from operations *and* value from customers early on. When synchronizing is not effective, the stair steps fragment, the digital initiatives don't connect, value creation is limited by silos, and the firm's progress toward future ready is stymied.

The lessons for creating value from operations and from customers that we described in chapters 3 and 4 apply to firms following pathway 3. However, the digital initiatives are typically smaller, faster, and more connected, with less time to learn.

Progressing on Pathway 3: DBS and KPN

Let's now look at case studies from two firms that have followed pathway 3 and successfully transformed—DBS, a financial services firm in Singapore, and KPN, a telecom provider in the Netherlands. DBS' choice of pathway 3 was partly driven by confidence that they could govern the switching focus from operational efficiency and customer experience and back again. The DBS case study focuses on its dominant organizational change (or explosion): the platform mindset. DBS synchronized many of the different activities on pathway 3 through reorganizing by platforms and took care of the other explosions along the way. In contrast, KPN was in a crisis mode and chose pathway 3 because they had to improve operational efficiency and customer experience at the same time. The KPN case study focuses on how the firm managed the four explosions to synchronize the initiatives.

DBS—Building the World's Best Bank, Synchronizing through Platforms

One way that firms have successfully synchronized on pathway 3 is by building and reusing platforms—creating firm-wide assets that can be connected together to create new value. DBS is a great example of a firm following pathway 3 and achieving outstanding financial performance.

DBS is a commercial bank headquartered in Singapore. It provides a full range of services in consumer, small, and medium enterprise (SME) and corporate banking, operating across eighteen markets. From 2009 to 2021, DBS moved from being described by some in Singapore as "damn bloody slow" to "the best bank in the world" by publications including *Euromoney*[2] and *Global Finance*.[3] DBS is one of the most remarkable turnarounds we have studied, and there are many lessons we can all learn. For more details, please see our DBS case studies written with Siew Kien Sia from the Nanyang School of Business in Singapore.[4]

The success of DBS' digital transformation lifted its bottom line and bolstered its reputation. Group total income rose from

$7.6 billion in 2014 to $12.4 billion in 2021.[5] The share price more than doubled from 2016 to 2018, with gains outstripping those of its main local rivals. *Euromoney* awarded DBS the World's Best Digital Bank in 2016 and again in 2018. In August 2018, DBS was named the "Best Bank in the World" by *Global Finance*. The magazine noted that DBS was "pointing the way to the future for the entire industry with its digital transformation."[6]

Threats posed by financial technology (fintech) disruption were relentless. At the same time, DBS also faced growing institutional constraints for organic expansion and acquisition-led growth in the region, specifically in the emerging Southeast Asia and South Asia markets. Instead of building banks the traditional way, DBS saw opportunities in leveraging technology to grow in these emerging markets.

The bank initiated its digital strategy in 2009 under the leadership of then-new CEO Piyush Gupta. Between 2009 and 2014, DBS invested heavily in technology and undertook radical changes to rewire the entire enterprise for digital innovation. Leaders used memorable terms to engage everyone in the firm in digital value creation. For example, becoming "Digital to the Core" (i.e., creating value from operations) and "Live More, Bank Less" (i.e., creating value from customers). Key steps of its digital transformation involved developing scalable digital platforms, revamping its technology and operations organization, leveraging technology to redesign its customer experience, and fostering internal as well as external digital innovation.

Becoming "Digital to the Core": Creating Value from Operations

The first priority was to rationalize and standardize the core technology platforms. DBS merged the technology division and operations division to form a new technology and operations division. David Gledhill, former chief information officer at DBS, describes DBS management's thinking:

> *Our belief is to get to the back-end, to sort out the pipes. This requires a vast amount of work in the back-end infrastructure, integration layers, messaging and all the associated innovations you need to make your architecture nimble. Getting the core right is where we really put our heavy spend. It will speed up the front-end. We build world-class systems on top of that.*[7]

DBS conducted a comprehensive diagnosis of its technological competencies, infrastructure, and emerging technology trends. A team also visited some of the world's foremost technology firms to glean valuable insights and learn how to implement industry-leading best practices in the bank. Gledhill observes:

> *We started to learn how the best technology organizations operate, how they engineer systems, how they think about customer experience, how they think about experimentation, how they move quickly. . . . We also learned about their culture and which cultural elements we could take on board. . . . The biggest aha moment for me was that none of these firms started out engineering things the way they ought to be. Not one. In fact, they all started out looking a lot like we looked. . . . They had big legacy systems, they had monoliths, and they weren't scalable. They couldn't move fast, and [so, they] had to change. Legacy debt, same story. If they could do it, so could we.*[8]

To be on par with technology firms, DBS built its delivery pipeline for scalability, speed-to-market, and continuous innovation. There was a huge push for virtualization as servers were decommissioned and data centers were shrunk. DBS instituted a policy of "everything goes to the cloud" and systematically sequenced its application migration from being cloud-ready to cloud-optimized and, eventually, cloud-native. They worked to automate as much as possible, using automation tools and optimizing the DevOps pipeline from testing to deployment to increase speed. They introduced new collaborative ways of working to speed up time to market and break down organizational silos.

Infrastructure engineering was rethought to be more service-oriented, pushing DevOps integration by removing the traditional separation between development and operations and strengthening the alignment of business and technology units. And finally, and perhaps most importantly, the emphasis was shifted from project to platform by moving from funding individual projects that needed approvals or subcommittee reviews to funding a group of business and technology people who jointly operate and manage key technology platforms.

A strategic decision was also made to bring DBS' technology infrastructure team in-house to run its own technology, moving from 85 percent outsourcing to 85 percent insourcing. According to Gledhill, "We just had to run our own technology, otherwise we'd never have our own technology DNA."[9]

The technology infrastructure, for example, was successfully insourced into a one-thousand-strong development center in India. One hundred percent of applications were on DevOps, and 80 percent were in the cloud (later up to about 95 percent), with 95 percent of systems being virtualized. DBS was able to cut its application costs by over 80 percent by the end of 2017. Its release cadence of new applications had increased close to ten times, thanks to pipeline automation for application development.[10]

"Live More, Bank Less": Creating Value from Customers

DBS also took its deeply ingrained customer journey philosophy to the next level by making banking invisible, captured in its "Live More, Bank Less" mantra. Lee Yan Hong, head of group human resources at DBS, noted, "Time is precious, so we want to give it back to the customers. When we make the bank invisible and customers' journeys joyful by putting all their banking needs on their phones, they have a 24x7 bank in their palms. The whole intent is to remove tedious customer tasks around banking."[11]

DBS' shift to embed banking into customer journeys was facilitated by a set of new key performance indicators (KPIs) that tracked value creation across five key areas:

- **Acquire**—increasing customer acquisition through wider online distribution (e.g., moving away from customer acquisition through branches or relationship managers toward digital marketing; HR accessing new talent pools through social media).

- **Transact**—eliminating paper and enabling instant fulfillment (e.g., moving away from physical documents to e-documents, such as consolidated e-statements; from manual account opening or trade execution to one-click straight-through processing or transaction automation).

- **Engage**—driving sticky customer behaviors and cross-selling through contextual marketing (e.g., personalized research reports served digitally; HR created a multipurpose app that allowed employees to connect, get all the "information on the go, work on the go, and connect on the go").[12]

- **Ecosystems**—embedding services in the customer journey, often by partnering with firms through APIs to deliver new customer value propositions. In November 2017, DBS rolled out its open API platform (among the world's largest API platforms hosted by a bank), offering over 150 APIs across more than twenty service categories such as fund transfers and real-time payments.[13] The platform was a way for developers and DBS to access each other's applications seamlessly. Most of these APIs facilitated business services, such as credit card management, calculation of loan eligibility, redemption of loyalty points, and calculation of foreign exchange rates.

- **Data**—using data to gain customer and operational insights. For example, DBS's automated teller machine (ATM) team worked with data scientists to create predictive models for preventive maintenance and cash recycling. This effort reduced ATM downtimes from 20 percent to a negligible level, saving the bank $20 million. Similarly, the bank's audit teams reaped considerable productivity gains by applying data analytics and machine learning to automate processes, such as branch risk profiling, trading fraud analysis, and credit risk assessment. HR also developed analytics models in recruitment, retention, and productivity assessment (e.g., to identify top traits of high performers, predict attrition, and implement their findings in the design of appropriate early intervention programs).

Synchronizing

DBS synchronized its digital initiatives to "become digital to the core" (create value from operations) and "live more, bank less" (create value from customers) by applying the four key elements we introduced earlier in the following ways.

MOTIVATE

To DBS, people were the key differentiator, and its aspiration was to nurture employees, embrace startup qualities, and "create a [then] 26,000-person start up"[14] to be customer-obsessed, data-driven, risk-taking, agile, and learning continually. The ambition to become "digital to the core" intensified once DBS compared itself to the best firms outside banking. To compete effectively, DBS wanted to be like the technology giants, including Google, Amazon, Netflix, Apple, LinkedIn, and Facebook. DBS aspired to be the D in the GANDALF. Gledhill observed:

> *GANDALF was an amazing rallying call to our people. It had a bigger impact on our people than anything else we have done, because it started to make them think about what was possible. It was an immediate culture pivot to shock people to think differently, like a lightning rod. Many of us have built our whole careers by doing things the old way. All of a sudden, we were told, that's different now. GANDALF was really what broke the glass for us and enabled us to describe a different way of running the firm without having to excuse the past.*[15]

DBS invested considerable resources in reskilling its people. In addition, the firm developed more flexible ways of working, such as allowing employees to join new teams working on innovative ideas on a part-time basis. Lee Yan Hong described the efforts:

> *Often when organizations undertake digital transformations, they focus on winning the "head" through vision and data-driven processes. Equally, if not more important, is winning the "heart." We must ensure employees are aligned on this journey by recognizing and appreciating their work and giving them opportunities to be the change and make a difference . . . We can't hope to be a big start-up with a digital culture while keeping everything centrally controlled. We have been working to enable empowerment throughout the organization, and we have seen that little things go a long way in changing the culture.[16]*

COORDINATE

As the digital transformation journey gained momentum, DBS recognized that its business strategies and technology strategies were becoming increasingly intertwined. It needed to further fuse business and technology through a new reorganization around technology platforms.

For DBS, a platform is a combination of technology assets and people that support, manage, and guide those technology assets, as well as its funding. DBS' list of platforms fell into four categories:

- **Business platforms** focused on customer-facing businesses, such as consumer banking business, enterprise banking business, and treasury and market business.

- **Enterprise shared platforms** supported multiple businesses with common services, such as customer data, payment, customer servicing, API development, and emerging technologies like artificial intelligence, blockchain, and chatbots.

- **Enterprise support platforms** were responsible for supporting functions that ran across all businesses, such as finance, HR, and core banking.

- **Enterprise enabling platforms** facilitated technology infrastructure, cybersecurity, access management, enterprise architecture, and delivery enablement.

Figure 5-1 shows the initial fourteen platforms at DBS. By 2021, the number of platforms has grown to thirty-three.[17]

5-1 DBS Reorganized by Platform

Banking Platforms

| Consumer | Institutional | Treasury | Wealth |

Enterprise Shared Platforms	Enterprise Support Platforms	Enterprise Enabling Platforms
Customer Data	Core Banking	Delivery Enablement
Customer Servicing	HR	Technology Infrastructure
Payment	Finance	Access Management
API Development	etc.	Cybersecurity
Emerging Technologies		etc.
etc.		

Source: Adapted from S. K. Sia, P. Weill, and M. Xu, Nanyang Technological University (The Asian Business Case Centre), and the MIT Center for Information Systems Research, "DBS: From the 'World's Best Bank' to Building the Future-Ready Enterprise," Case Ref No. ABCC-2019-001, December 2018.

Incentives and decision-making processes had to be realigned. To facilitate the change, DBS established a two-in-a-box system to govern these platforms.[18] Bidyut Dumra, head of innovation at DBS, said:

> From a governance perspective, we wanted to pursue a two-in-a-box approach. That's related to the entire notion of us wanting to operate in the guise of a start-up. In a start-up, the two main people are the CEO and the CTO. The business and technology are joined. If you're a digital business, those two have to be synced. So, for every platform, we have a business and a technology lead. These two people make all the decisions for that entire platform: they have joint KPIs, so they are both delivering one dream.[19]

PRIORITIZE

In the new platform organization, with its two-in-a-box governance model, a technology lead for a business platform shared responsibility for the P&L, while a business lead shared responsibility for technology KPIs and technology support budgets, which would be treated as business expenses. This reorganization around the platform took the fusion between business and technology to a new level. It operated on a single backlog prioritization model. Bidyut Dumra, head of innovation at DBS, described the change:

> The business and the technology backlogs have come together. For example, with HR, the intent on the business side might be to automate the talent search process and the onboarding process—those are items in the business

backlog. From a technology perspective, they might have a backlog item like needing to upgrade the PeopleSoft software or a hardware upgrade. You can see that those are two separate backlogs. Now mesh those together, and work on them with the same pool of people. . . . With these backlogs coming together, the relationship is changing; the dependency and the conversations are changing to the point where we say the intent is that "business equals technology" and "technology equals business."[20]

INNOVATE

DBS' efforts to create value from operations and from customers (become digital to the core and embed banking in customer journeys), supported by its reskilling initiatives, provided the fertile ground for continuous experimentation and business innovation. More than two thousand experiments and innovation projects were launched in 2017. In particular, the launch of digibank, DBS' mobile-only bank in India, in April 2016 was a bold step in its experimentation with new banking concepts. Digibank was paperless, signatureless, and branchless. A customer's identity was verified using his/her national biometric ID. Customer service was delivered by an AI-driven virtual assistant, which handled over 80 percent of all customer requests without human intervention.[21] Digibank required just a fifth of the resources of a traditional bank setup; it was thus able to compete aggressively by offering consumers higher interest rates and lower banking fees. Banking without branches, ATMs, or bank managers, digibank India gained one million customers in the first year.[22]

DBS also learned to sharpen its external partnering capability, creating value from ecosystems as it developed its digital ecosystem around customer needs. One example was its partnership with

Tally, the largest enterprise resource planning (ERP) vendor for SMEs in India. The API integration with Tally's ERP enabled DBS to offer instant financial products like loans to SMEs with healthy transaction flows when they ran low in their cash position.

In summary, Piyush Gupta, CEO, describes DBS' transformation:

> *I have to confess: it's not always clear that you can call the future. But it is clear that you must have a point of view on the future. You want to make sure that you have thought about it enough such that you have enough ideas to be able to be adaptive and to be responsive. The winner over the next 10 to 12 years will be people who have been able to build nimbleness, flexibility, adaptability, and responsiveness into their way of working.*[23]

KPN—Managing Explosions to Transform Iteratively

We now turn to KPN, the largest Dutch telco.[24] The firm was facing a severe competitive situation in 2014. KPN followed pathway 3, achieving significant improvements by 2018 and beyond. In this case study, we will focus on how KPN iterated back and forth between digital initiatives that focused on creating value from customers and value from operations and how they handled the four explosions to successfully transform.

KPN is a provider of information and communications technology services in the Netherlands, serving consumer and business markets with a range of products that include mobile and broadband connectivity and cloud services. Today, KPN's ambition is: "We want to make the Netherlands the most connected country in the world. We want to lead the country's digitalization and become the preferred partner in digital life."[25] Reflecting on their transformation journey in the 2020 annual report, KPN noted, "Since the start of the latest strategic program in 2019, we have become a much leaner, faster and simpler firm. . . . We have built a strong foundation for the years to come."[26]

Seven years earlier, however, KPN was under significant financial strain. Strong competition had reduced prices in saturated markets, regulations had capped termination rates and roaming fees, and over-the-top firms,[27] such as WhatsApp, Skype, Spotify, and Netflix, had eroded legacy revenue streams (from voice and text) while placing a heavy burden on network capacity.[28]

KPN needed to improve both its operational efficiency and customer experience nearly simultaneously to remain competitive, making pathway 3 its best option. At the start of the transformation, a few customer experience initiatives—such as creating a single customer identity for digital services and improving the order capture process—seemed especially promising, with large potential returns. Unfortunately, KPN's distributed (and mostly outsourced) IT capabilities restricted the firm from immediately executing these initiatives: "Our capabilities were horrible. We had outsourced, offshored way too much. . . . If we really wanted to make the dream of a digital telco come true, then we had to build the capabilities ourselves," said Bouke Hoving, former chief information officer, KPN.[29]

Before KPN could pursue the goal of creating a better customer experience, it had to make several improvements to its operational foundation—first, moving to the right (increase operational efficiency) on its pathway before moving up (enhance customer experience).

The process started with changes in decision rights. The CIO obtained a mandate from the CEO to form a transformation unit called simplification and innovation (S&I), in which he could centralize all business process redesign, IT architecture, and IT development capabilities. As a result, all commercial business unit directors had to give up (much of) their individual change rights, and the CIO put all localized back-end transformations (which had mostly been outsourced) on hold. This freed up significant amounts of capital and helped shift the focus toward creating new ways of working that could deliver new customer solutions.

Bringing developers and designers in-house energized innovation and brought IT development closer to the business. S&I relied on specialized external firms to recruit magnets—the very best digital talent who had the power to draw other talent into the firm—to work at KPN. The unit also relocated from KPN's headquarters in The Hague to Amsterdam—a location that would be more attractive to an international candidate base—where it created a new and exciting digital workplace. The difference was more than physical—new hires initiated a shift away from traditional processing systems to open-source and cloud-based environments and worked in agile teams. This new way of working, internally referred to as "digital craftsmanship," enabled more collective work habits, experimentation, and the development of the teams' craft.

Embedding these agile practices in the existing corporate governance proved challenging because S&I's new way of working did not map to KPN's traditional reporting policies and management mechanisms: "The biggest explosion was our internal target to cancel all the steering committees, KPI spreadsheets, internal management letters, management layers, and also the corporate appraisal system—which were all big inhibitors for our staff," explained Bouke Hoving. S&I's leadership appointed proxies, individuals who maintained tight communication lines with the rest of the firm and ensured that S&I adhered to KPN's standard reporting requirements.[30] This eliminated unnecessary overhead for the agile teams, allowing them to learn (without fear of negative performance evaluations) from mistakes occurring during the agile development process.

The changes initiated by KPN's new talent had a positive effect on the firm's platform mindset and bottom line. KPN decommissioned 25 percent of its systems while replacing every legacy platform and phasing out traditional software, replacing it with open-source and cloud-based environments. Early in the transformation, S&I's agile teams developed a digital engine that enabled API access to over three hundred legacy services from KPN's back end, allowing developers to quickly realize new customer-oriented initiatives. For instance, one of the first digital engine projects redesigned the process to reduce the instore order capture time for KPN's popular quad-play bundle of services from thirty minutes to three minutes—a major breakthrough in customer experience.

S&I's goal was to show results early and often, thus demonstrating transformation momentum. Only after initial improvements to customer experience had been made did S&I set its sights on a greenfield transformation of KPN's operational backbone. A next-generation business support system was introduced, further improving the APIs and enabling a second wave of customer experience improvements. Before S&I migrated customers to the new operational backbone, it worked closely with the commercial consumer unit to help rationalize KPN's product portfolio. Together, the two units initiated organizational surgery, starting with a two-year commercial product freeze. During this time, they cut 80 percent of KPN's product offerings and harmonized processes among the remaining products. This massive simplification effort helped to break down internal silos and solidified the firm's change of focus from products to the customer.

From 2014 to 2018, KPN's digital business transformation created significant value from operations, reducing downtime by 90 percent and achieving €570 million (US $622 million) in savings (90 percent above the original target). Perhaps more importantly, the firm strongly improved its customer experience—achieving an NPS improvement of twenty points. This helped create more value from customers—recruiting new ones and retaining existing ones. By mid-2018, KPN was ready to lead innovation in the 5G era.

To help manage the four explosions in your firm, figure 5-2 summarizes our interpretation of how the four explosions were handled at KPN—particularly how they helped synchronize the activities on pathway 3.

The Future at KPN

Like all businesses, KPN was impacted by the outbreak of Covid-19 in 2019. Fortunately, their transformation helped set them up to deal with this unprecedented set of challenges. Joost Farwerck, CEO and chairman of KPN, reflected on the future in the 2020 annual report:

> *We will shift our firm's way of working to a more hybrid model that will reduce our office footprint, combining remote working with collaboration, brainstorming and socializing in an inspiring office environment. . . . I believe that continued and consistent digitalization and simplification will create a more effective and flexible organization. Our purpose-led performance and digitally savvy workforce are key to our ongoing efforts.*[31]

5-2 How KPN Dealt with Explosions

🪁 Decision Rights

- Obtained transformation mandate from CEO
- Centralized all business process redesign, IT architecture, and IT development capabilities from business units into the firm's digital unit

🔄 New Ways of Working

- Re-insourced front-end talent for the creation of 250 "agile to the max" (autonomous, cross-functional, empowered) teams
- Focused on employee craftsmanship and continuous learning; became customer oriented and data-driven
- Canceled nearly all official reporting and appraisal mechanisms

🪁 Platform Mindset

- Developed an API-enabled digital engine to make legacy services available to every developer
- Created infrastructure and platform team that moved KPN toward open source plus its own cloud solution, and challenged developers to automate when possible
- Replaced IT spaghetti with one new (and simplified) back-end system

🩺 Organizational Surgery

- Collapsed business silos by taking out 80% of products and harmonizing processes
- Removed 90% of managers in the digital unit

Source: Interviews with company executives; company documents.

What Leaders Should Focus On

To successfully lead a transformation on pathway 3 requires articulating a vision of what your future-ready firm looks like and how leadership will engage everyone to improve both customer experience and operational efficiency at about the same time. But even more importantly, leadership must synchronize all the moving parts along the pathway 3 journey. The most challenging element is picking the right projects for each stage of the stair steps, delivering value from those projects, and coordinating across. Picking the right projects is typically not about the highest short-term return on investment or having the best salesperson present them. Instead, it's about crafting projects that build on one another to alternatively create value from customers and operations and lay a foundation for the future. Then ensuring that the value from the previous projects plugs into the next project to continue the firm's journey to becoming future ready.

Coordinating the activities of a large firm while it alternates focus on operational efficiency and customer experience is also a big challenge of a pathway 3 transformation and the most likely cause of failure. DBS used the creation and reuse of platforms as a vehicle to coordinate all the activities of their transformation. DBS reorganized the firm by platforms and adopted a two-in-the-box governance approach. Other firms use different approaches to coordination, for example, relying on the four explosions. KPN focused heavily on effectively managing the new ways of working and changing decision rights to coordinate their transformation efforts.

For leaders embarking on pathway 3, figure 5-3 proposes an order in which to focus on value and explosions. As with all pathways, leaders have to start by aligning decision rights to the pathway. For pathway 3, power must be given to the leaders who prioritize what projects the firm will undertake and which ones they will pass on or leave for later. A unique feature of pathway 3 is that leaders focus on creating value from operations and customers in the first year. Most firms achieve this task by creating a vision, picking key projects, and then creating a dashboard to measure value and change incentives to target the desired value.

Firms traveling on the early upward sections of the stair steps need to focus on new ways of working to create value from customers quickly, as we saw in both KPN and DBS. When the firm moves horizontally on the stair steps, the initial focus is on creating

5-3 Pathway 3—What Leaders Should Focus On

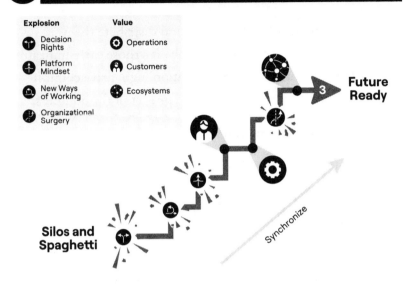

Source: The posited order of the actions results from our qualitative research. We tested our hypothesis that decision rights was the explosion to anticipate and manage first using hierarchical regression equations and the data from the MIT CISR 2019 Top Management Teams and Transformation Survey (N = 1,311).

platforms that capture the crown jewels of the firm and make them reusable during later steps. Typically, further along the stair steps, firms reorganize to move faster toward becoming future ready and begin capturing more value from ecosystems. These new goals also need to be captured in the dashboards and incentive changes.

Action Items from Chapter 5

The first three actions are common to every transformation.

1. Communicate today (and every day) that your firm is focusing on a pathway 3 transformation to become future ready. Paint a picture of what working in the firm will look

like in the future and articulate the steps along the way to help people understand their roles.

2. Collect stories of early success and distribute them widely—internally and externally. It's those early indicators of success that help keep motivation high, drive commitment and progress, and stem the impact of the doubters.

3. Create a plan for managing the explosions.

4. As part of your firm's communication plan about proceeding on pathway 3, give a preview of what this transformation will feel like, describing the shorter-term (six to twelve months in duration) initiatives that will alternate in focus from improving customer experience to increasing operational efficiency and back again. Your people will depend on this road map to guide their attention and activities.

5. Focus on synchronizing projects along the stair steps. This consists of picking key projects that can deliver real value in a relatively short timeframe, accumulating the value, and then passing on the lessons learned to the next project so that cumulative learning and progress occur.

6. Be aware of the whiplash that can happen on pathway 3 because of the short-term iterative nature of the projects that make up the transformation. You will need to implement strong communication and governance to change focus depending on where your firm is in the transformation.

7. Track metrics about value from both operations and customers and perhaps value from ecosystems. This is one of the harder tasks to get right in a pathway 3 transformation.

Identify, if possible, metrics that accomplish both (or in the best of all worlds, all three).

8. Review the DBS and KPN examples to identify good ideas that can be adjusted to align with your firm's culture.

Chapter 6

Pathway 4

Create a New Unit

What do you do when your firm doesn't have the time to transform to take advantage of a new digital business opportunity or defend against a serious digital threat? You create a new born-digital unit designed to succeed—with the right people, the new business model, the enabling culture, and the best partners and platforms. Building these new units is the fourth pathway to becoming future ready. For many firms, a pathway 4 initiative implements a new business model and is often part of a transformation with (hopefully) well-coordinated multiple pathways. For example, an insurance firm could follow pathway 1 to industrialize their core business, automating claims and improving the customer experience. At the same time, the firm can also create a pathway 4 unit with a new ecosystem business model to become a go-to destination for home security and integrate their insurance products and partner services, such as alarm systems, fencing, and lighting, all under a new brand targeted at millennials and sold only on an app.

Here are some successful pathway 4 initiatives:

- **Climate FieldView by Bayer:** The Bayer subsidiary Climate LLC offers a go-to destination for farmers to manage the yield per square meter of their crops with the FieldView platform—helping farmers focus on their goals (rather than only inputs like herbicides and seeds).[1] Their purpose is "a digital agriculture ecosystem where farmers, globally, can easily access a broad and interconnected set of tools, services, and data to optimize all of their decisions on the farm."[2] Climate integrates more than seventy partner offerings, including satellite imaging, sensors, drones, weather information, prescription planting software, insurance, and other offerings, into its subscription-based service.[3] The digital agriculture business, launched in 2015, has grown to more than 180 million farming acres globally in 2020.[4] The pathway 4 unit is one key initiative for Bayer's crop science division to achieve its goal of outcomes-based, digitally enabled solutions. In November 2021, Bayer announced a partnership with Microsoft Azure to scale the FieldView platform and develop a digital platform to advance agricultural sustainability for a broader ecosystem, including firms in the food industry.[5]

- **Ping An Good Doctor:** China's largest insurer, Ping An, created the Good Doctor platform, which offers a 24-7 go-to destination for healthcare services that are provided by a growing ecosystem of 189,000 pharmacies, 4,000 hospitals, 1,700 checkup centers, and over 1,800 medical institutions (as of September 30, 2021), and an inhouse medical team of 2,000, whose services are coordinated through AI physician assistants. In 2021, the platform had more than 400 million registered users (an increase of 55 million users from 2020) and 740,000 paid users from corporate healthcare customers.[6] The firm recorded revenue of RMB3.818 billion (approximately US $605 million),[7] an increase of 39 percent from the previous year.[8] In 2021, Ping An Good Doctor also announced a new growth strategy, including new customer offerings like a family doctor membership and a business model targeting online healthcare users, healthcare providers, and corporate healthcare users.[9]

- **next by Bradesco:** next by Bradesco is a digital platform that aims to make people's lives easier and encourages them to achieve their goals. next was launched in 2017 as the digital bank of Bradesco. In 2022, it operates as a digital platform, with Bradesco as its main investor and has more than 10 million customers. It attributes its growth to the focus on customers, attentive listening to their needs, and understanding trends and behaviors through analytical data. In addition to financial services (checking accounts, salary accounts, debit and credit cards, insurance options, investments, and loans), next offers nonfinancial solutions. They include nextShop (a retail marketplace with offers and online cashback); a nextJoy account for children and teenagers, in partnership with Disney; online streaming services; and integration with digital wallets.[10]

- **Nequi:** Bancolombia's pathway 4 initiative, Nequi, was the first digital bank in Colombia.[11] The startup was created in Bancolombia's innovation lab in 2014 with two goals: (1) attract the unbanked to Bancolombia, and help those customers deal with money (e.g., through simple language and metaphors such as "pockets" and "saving money under the mattress" to make users feel more comfortable) and (2) become a test laboratory for Bancolombia's traditional banking business. For example, Bancolombia tested part of its ecosystem strategy through Nequi by experimenting with application programming interfaces (APIs) to develop partnerships. Those learnings were eventually integrated into Bancolombia's operations. Nequi's long-term prospects—remain a business unit or become a separate business—were not clear until the Covid-19 pandemic, and the resulting government distribution of aid, transformed Nequi's user base. By the end of 2021, Nequi had over 10 million customers, and they were more diverse than had been anticipated. In December 2021, the Bancolombia board of directors authorized Nequi to operate as a 100 percent digital credit firm—a separate business from Bancolombia, with its own financial license.

Why Follow Pathway 4 and What to Expect

About 10 percent of all the firms we studied adopted pathway 4 as their dominant approach to becoming future ready. In addition, many of the 22 percent of firms adopting multiple pathways have a pathway 4 initiative. Pathway 4 was commonly adopted by firms in the consumer, financial services, manufacturing, and heavy industries. Firms in mining, oil, and gas, education, and telecom/media industries were the least likely to adopt pathway 4 journeys.

The need for speed to market typically drives firms to undertake a pathway 4 transformation, fueled by the firms' leaders' perception that a significant portion of their revenues over the next five years is under threat. Firms following pathway 4 estimated that 43 percent of their revenues would be lost in five years if they didn't change compared to 26 percent, 39 percent, and 37 percent for firms following pathways 1, 2, or 3, respectively. Pathway 4 firms often believe there is an attractive new business model opportunity that will require a different approach than is possible within their main business.

Pathway 4 transformations are all about creating a future-ready unit that's born digital from day one. This opportunity makes pathway 4 exciting—the firm is testing and learning without an established playbook, which would be much harder to do in the main business. In our research, we found there are four questions executives in firms on a pathway 4 journey must answer—but often don't.

What Is the Business Model?

A key question to ask in any digital initiative, and more importantly in a pathway 4 transformation, is: What is the proposed business model? In our 2018 Harvard Business Review Press book *What's Your Digital Business Model?* we described the four different ways companies can make money in the digital era.[12] In our workshops with senior executives about their most important digital transformation initiatives, we found that most large firms are exploring four business models on two dimensions, the depth of knowledge of their end customer and the firm business design (see figure 6-1). Most large firms have revenues from more than one of the business models. Each of the four business models is profitable on average, though their risk and reward profiles differ—and firms often operate more than one model. We list the models from highest to lowest industry-adjusted average growth rates.

- **Ecosystem Driver:** Firms that are the go-to destination for their customers by offering their own services plus curated

6-1 Four Digital Business Models

Complete Knowledge of Your End Customer

Omnichannel

- Own customer relationship
- Create multiproduct customer experience to address customer jobs to be done
- Offer a choice of channels and customers choose
- Leverage an integrated value chain

  e.g., banks, retail, utilities

Ecosystem Driver

- Become the go-to destination in your domain
- Add complementary and possibly competitor products
- Ensure great customer experience
- Match customer needs with providers
- Acquire customer data from all interactions
- Extract rents

  e.g., Amazon, Fidelity, Domain

Value Chain ←———————————————→ **Ecosystem**

Supplier

- Focus on low-cost production and incremental innovation as core skills
- Risk losing power

  e.g., manufacturers, pharmaceuticals

Modular Producer

- Adaptable to any ecosystem
- Innovate constantly

  e.g., PayPal, Okta, Klarna

Partial Knowledge of Your End Customer

Source: Weill, P., and Woerner, S. L.,. *What's Your Digital Business Model? Six Questions to Help You Build the Next-Generation Enterprise* (Boston: Harvard Business Review Press, 2018).

complementary offers from partners. Examples include Amazon, TradeLens, Climate FieldView, and Domain.

- **Modular Producer:** Firms that provide plug-and-play services that adapt to a variety of ecosystems. These businesses are typically based on digital platforms with a set of API-enabled services and are technology agnostic. Examples include PayPal, Kabbage, part of Fidelity, and Okta.

- **Omnichannel:** Firms that provide customers with access to their own services across multiple channels, aiming to seamlessly combine physical and digital experiences. Examples of this model include most large retailers and banks.

- **Supplier:** Firms that provide their products in the value chain of another company. Suppliers don't typically have a strong relationship with the end customer and struggle with cross-selling. Suppliers include many manufacturers, many pharmaceutical firms, as well as some insurance firms, banks, and firms selling investment products.

In recent years, only the ecosystem driver and modular producer business models have both growth and margins above their industry averages.[13] The other two models, while still profitable, have growth and profit margins below their industry average, and we expect this trend will strengthen in the next decade. Although occasionally we do see pathway 4 initiatives implementing supplier and omnichannel business models (e.g., business units launching in a new country), most initiatives we have seen and studied are targeting ecosystem driver or modular producer business models.

What Is the Target Customer Domain?

The critical question for any firm contemplating an ecosystem driver model is: What do we want to become the go-to destination for? Like Amazon, TradeLens, or Domain, the answer may become more ambitious as the ecosystem becomes more successful. For decades, companies have thought of themselves as operating in industries such as banking, retail, shipping, automotive, and energy. In contrast, most customers have (often cross-industry) needs and problems that must be solved—for example, business customers want to manage their energy consumption, and consumers want to get an education, buy a house, or manage their daily lives. We call these customer problems *domains*.[14] This mismatch often results in a fragmented customer experience. An ecosystem business model rethinks how to solve customer needs in each of their important domains.

For example, in serving its business-to-business customers, Schneider Electric moved from selling discrete products to connected energy solutions, addressing the customer domain for managing energy needs. The result is that over 50 percent of Schneider's revenue comes from Internet of Things–enabled digital solutions.[15] The firm's best customers now realize 65 percent energy efficiency, compared to the average business energy efficiency of 30 percent.[16] Similarly, Fidelity expanded their curated set of partner offerings to provide complementary, unique value based on its in-depth knowledge of customers. For example, for the life event of sending a child to college, Fidelity combines its own products, such as mutual funds, with partner products, like student loan refinancing through Credible.[17]

To stimulate your thinking about domains versus industries, figure 6-2 shows the percent of firms from various industries participating in the customer domain for home. The key insight is that successfully delivering on a customer domain requires integrating offerings from many different industries. The winner could come from any participating industry or even be a born-digital company designed to serve a customer domain.

6-2 Domains Can Include Many Industries

Housing Domain
Percentage of Firms by Industry

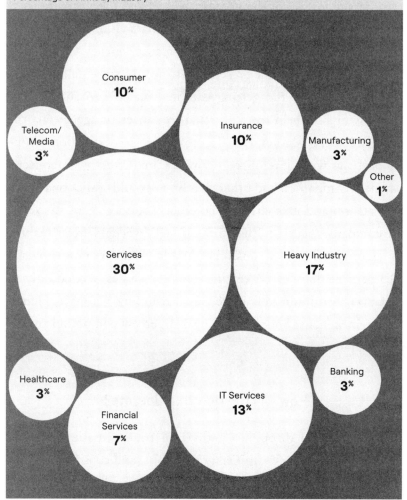

Consumer
10%

Telecom/
Media
3%

Insurance
10%

Manufacturing
3%

Other
1%

Services
30%

Heavy Industry
17%

Healthcare
3%

Financial
Services
7%

IT Services
13%

Banking
3%

Source: MIT CISR 2019 Top Management Teams and Transformation Survey (N = 1,311). Respondents were asked to choose one dominant domain for their organization. The domains are based on data collected in the MIT CISR 2017 Ecosystem Survey (N = 158) and ten of the twelve McKinsey categories described in "Competing in a World of Sectors without Borders," by Venkat Atluri, Miklós Dietz, and Nicolaus Henke, in *McKinsey Quarterly*, July 12, 2017 (digital content and public services were omitted). Industries are based on NAICS categories.

Shopify exemplifies a firm shaped around a customer domain rather than an industry.[18] Shopify CEO Tobi Lütke set out to start an online snowboard shop, building the e-commerce software to support it. In the process, he realized the software itself would be a more promising venture. Shopify's vision is deceptively simple: supporting the entire online retailer journey—building a brand, creating an online presence, setting up a store, selling, marketing, managing, and getting educated on how to run a small business or hire help from a vetted freelancer or agency via the Shopify Experts Marketplace. To grow its go-to destination, Shopify partners with developers, designers, marketers, warehousers, payment companies, and others. As Shopify adds functionality to its platform and its share of e-commerce services grows, so will the company's access to the transactional-level data it can analyze to identify additional customer needs. Shopify now holds a 10.3 percent share of US retail e-commerce sales, second only to Amazon. A million-plus merchants, including Walmart, Heinz, and Heineken, use Shopify, fueling a 41 percent compound annual growth rate.[19]

How Will the New Unit Operate?

Being successful through a pathway 4 transformation requires focus on value from customers, operations, and ecosystems from day one. This means that the pathway 4 transformation really must hit the ground running and create a lot of the value early on.

To enable rapid success, digital transformation leaders face many decisions about how the new unit will operate, including: How will the new unit be branded, resourced, and managed? Will the new unit use services provided by the parent firm, such as HR, legal, IT, marketing, or even some existing products? Will it target the firm's existing customers or a new demographic like millennials or small businesses? What are the key new capabilities that need to be built? And finally, will the new unit be a separate business, a business unit of the firm, a joint venture, or some other model? This leads to the final question.

What Will You Do if the New Unit Is Successful?

Pathway 4 initiatives are designed to improve both customer experience and operational efficiency faster than their parent unit. The mismatch between the dramatically improved customer experience and operational efficiency in the new unit compared to that of the parent unit ultimately creates the dilemma of how to integrate the two businesses (and cultures and systems) down the road. If successful, should the pathway 4 unit continue to operate separately, perhaps slowly cannibalizing the main business? Should customers of the traditional business move over to the new business unit? Or should the new business be spun out to survive on its own? This is a challenging decision to make before the unit is launched but well worth considering. Here are some options we have seen:

- Move customers from the firm to the new unit over time or vice versa (e.g., ING had great success launching ING Direct in 1989, then rebranding it to ING in 2017 and integrating it into the main business).

- Running the new unit as a separate business (e.g., Climate FieldView, TradeLens, Nequi).

- Spinning off the new unit by selling it or IPO'ing it (e.g., Domain).

A pathway 4 transformation is more than just about an innovation project; it's a substantial investment in how the firm will make money in the future.

Progressing on Pathway 4:
TradeLens and Domain

Let's now look at two pathway 4 transformations in more detail. Maersk, one of the largest global transport and logistics companies, developed a successful platform, TradeLens, with strategic partner IBM, to create value in global shipping by facilitating information-sharing and removing inefficiencies. Fairfax Media developed Domain to help customers manage the entire property journey. It was eventually IPO'ed, creating substantial new value (for Fairfax and others), and operates today as a listed company.

TradeLens: Transforming Data-Sharing
in Global Shipping

A. P. Moller–Maersk (Maersk) is a global transport and logistics company operating in 130 countries, growing substantially during the Covid-19 pandemic to $62 billion in 2021 revenues.[20] In 2017, Maersk began a digital transformation from a port-to-port ocean carrier to an integrated logistics company. The goal of one digital initiative—the global trade digitization (GTD) initiative— was to create value by resolving inefficiencies for ocean carriers and their customers (i.e., shippers and freight forwarders) by sharing information about supply chain events and trade documents using blockchain. The shipping industry is very fragmented and characterized by high costs and complexity, inefficiencies and delays, risk of fraud, high uncertainty, data security concerns, and disputes—a tough environment, particularly for smaller players.[21]

Some of these challenges result from the industry having many, many participants and a myriad of point-to-point solutions. These complex industries are great opportunities for an ecosystem solution—a go-to destination—that would manage all container information and beyond for a customer.[22] Maersk and IBM created a blockchain-based platform with an API layer for ecosystem participants—a nice technological solution for this problem, as it would enable everyone to see the same information quickly, removing potential inequities and errors from multiple systems with the same data.

Creating a go-to destination requires significant changes and experimentation. Changes in decision rights and organizational surgery were the key explosions for this very successful pathway 4 effort. Maersk and strategic partner IBM developed the platform in a collaboration and launched a commercial solution named TradeLens in December 2018. Some firms were concerned that in joining the platform, they would be sharing valuable data with competitors. Maersk established a new unit—the subsidiary GTD Solution Inc.—and the two partners advanced the blockchain solution (e.g., with trust anchors and the channel architecture) to help alleviate this concern.

GTD Solution Inc. continues the strategic partnership with IBM through the TradeLens collaboration team, with the two firms making joint decisions on the development of the platform and ecosystem. Positioned as a neutral platform, TradeLens is growing fast. In March 2021, TradeLens had three hundred ecosystem participants (up from 175 in 2020) and covered more than 50 percent of global shipping container volume.[23] By March 2022, over one thousand participants had joined the platform, with more than two-thirds of global shipping represented on the platform.[24]

The TradeLens platform focused on creating all three kinds of value from the beginning, with different priorities. The first priority is to create new value from operations by digitizing events and trade documents. The value proposition for partners to join the ecosystem is operational efficiency through more visibility of events and reduced costs from access to digital bills of lading, as provided by the TradeLens electronic bill of lading (eBL) solution. The firm tracks net value capture, which includes direct and indirect benefits (e.g., reduced working capital requirements, improved compliance). A key outcome so far is $120 net value creation per bill of lading issued, which includes direct and indirect benefits from easy access to container information.

The second priority is capturing more value from customers through partnering. TradeLens' number of customers and usage are increasing. The platform had one hundred customers in November 2020 through its three digital offerings—the core offering and two applications related to the bill of lading (the eBL and one for trade financiers). In December 2020, Maersk CEO Søren Skou said, "In the coming year, we will see actual revenue growth in TradeLens. . . . [The venture] is heading into a new phase where we truly have something we can sell."[25] The platform is also enabling new customers, in particular smaller companies, to join international trade.[26]

The big opportunity is to become the go-to destination for shippers. In 2020, TradeLens reached a major milestone: five of the largest ocean carriers had joined the platform.[27] These strong partners can influence their networks to grow the ecosystem. At the same time, GTD Solution Inc. began to partner with software companies for inland transportation. The subsidiary's next goals are achieving a critical mass of trade financing banks and custom authorities in the TradeLens ecosystem and developing a third-party marketplace.

To create value from TradeLens, GTD Solution has developed its platform mindset, a key differentiator, by defining and connecting three layers: products, platform, and ecosystem.

- **Products:** The most important requirement for starting this venture was the business case for creating commercially viable offerings. TradeLens started with a few targeted applications, selling access to digitized events and trade documents, that created value for Maersk and Maersk customers. GTD Solution Inc. focused on building the core set of functionalities and enabling innovation.

- **Platform:** TradeLens sought to offer the best technology, data, and support, including open APIs (instead of electronic data interchange), the blockchain and permission structure for security and transparency, and integration support with legacy systems.

- **Ecosystem:** TradeLens' ecosystem success depended on growing the network. GTD Solution focuses on delivering a new industry model with an end-to-end focus, while other platforms have limited scope. Activities have included adding strong partners who can help grow the network (as the ocean carriers), creating a customer advisory board, and collaborating on industry standards.

TradeLens has become a remarkable success in a very short time. With about half of the global shipping of containers currently tracked by the firm, it is slowly adding important complementary services like trade financing to its offerings. As the

TradeLens ecosystem achieves critical mass, the potential for increasing value captured from ecosystems is high.

Domain: Becoming a Go-to Destination for the Housing Journey

Domain Group is an Australian real estate media and technology services business with a portfolio of brands.[28] Starting in the late 1990s as a print and online real estate classified ads subsidiary of Fairfax Media (a media conglomerate), Domain, the initial company (and now a brand) in the Domain Group, has since become a go-to destination to inform, inspire, and connect consumers and real estate agents throughout the property life cycle, including partner offerings for home loans, insurance, and residential utility connections.

Domain was created as a go-to destination for both buyers and agents. The pathway 4 firm identified five steps in the housing journey: dreaming, searching, buying, settlement, and post-move-in that defines their customer domain, with services at each step. For example, for the buying step, Domain partnered with thirty-five mortgage providers to be a one-stop shop for getting a mortgage. It also provided home contents or landlord insurance in this step. Domain has become very successful, reaching 9.6 million Australians in a month out of a total population of 25 million.[29]

Domain Group became a publicly listed company on the Australian stock exchange in November 2017, creating A\$0.75 billion (US \$0.5 billion) in new value for majority shareholder Fairfax Media on its first day of trading. Such separation is an attractive strategy for parent companies that have successfully followed pathway 4, though this was not the initial goal of Fairfax Media.

Robyn Elliott, former chief information officer, Fairfax Media, explains: "We didn't decide immediately that [Domain] would be separate. What we decided was they should be separable. From a technology point of view, you want to create strategic options; you don't want technology to be a thing that holds back your strategy."[30]

The digital transformation of Domain started in 2012. As one of the many subsidiaries of Fairfax Media, it was regarded as a classified ads marketplace extension of Fairfax's publishing business. This meant it faced the same operational efficiency and cost-cutting imperatives as the rest of the company, which was grappling with declining revenues across the media landscape.

Although Domain slowly grew its customer base, which helped to offset declining publishing revenues, it also lagged behind industry leader Real Estate Australia (REA). Staying competitive required significant investments—most notably in its technology infrastructure. The management committee decided that Domain should operate as a standalone entity to accelerate its development and enhance its flexibility. Because Domain's sales and customer culture fundamentally differed from its parent's editorial culture, creating a separate unit made the most sense.

Domain's transformation journey started with three types of nearly simultaneous organizational explosions—decision rights, organizational surgery, and new ways of working (see figure 6-3 for a summary of how the explosions were handled at Domain).

Corporate restructuring made Domain a standalone division within Fairfax Media, alongside divisions such as Australian Publishing Media, Digital Ventures, and Fairfax Radio. The new division had its own executive team, which included a newly hired and entrepreneurial CEO and a chief technology officer.

6-3 How Domain Dealt with Explosions

Decision Rights

- Appointed a separate executive team including a newly hired CEO and CTO
- Negotiated ability to make decisions locally on strategy, technology, and scaling

New Ways of Working

- Promoted a sales culture, divergent from its parent's publishing and content heritage
- Implemented test-and-learn approaches to support fast digital product life cycles
- Treated data on how consumers interact with products as a strategic asset

Platform Mindset

- Focused on the broader ecosystem for the entire property journey
- Replatformed a mobile-centric solution using microservices to reduce unit costs and encourage plug-and-play partnerships

Organizational Surgery

- Was created as a standalone division to accelerate development, with access to corporate back-office systems to leverage expertise
- Was designed to be separable from parent firm but not necessarily separate
- Eventually spun out from parent firm and was listed on Australia's stock exchange

Source: Interviews with company executives; company documents.

Together, they negotiated local decision rights, most notably for the technology infrastructure. The intention was for Domain to pursue its own strategies while still providing scaling benefits to—and leveraging relevant centralized capabilities from—its corporate parent.

Fairfax Media's cloud-based architecture meant that costs were variable, allowing for flexible technology recharge. Rather than drawing on external consultants, Domain relied on Fairfax Media for back-office expertise, such as HR and internal auditing. In terms of adopting new ways of working, Domain drew heavily on its sales-oriented culture. In a few months, the two-hundred-person unit was living and breathing digital product life cycles and bringing new features to market using test-and-learn approaches. Domain's dedicated director of employee experience focused on fostering work habits geared to innovation and progress. Over the next five years, these new ways of working enabled Domain to rapidly scale up its sales, product development, and technology teams to approximately 850 employees.

With the right strategy, structure, agreements, funding, processes, and work habits in place, Domain could then focus on its key differentiator—a platform mindset. Initially, the goal was to develop an innovative, mobile-centric customer solution that would serve as the go-to destination for both prospective home buyers and real estate agents. However, as Domain gained a better understanding of its customer base (i.e., consumers and agents), it focused on creating a broader ecosystem for the home customer domain—the entire property journey from first dreaming of a house to settlement and post-move-in. To achieve this, Domain replatformed to lighter, purpose-built technologies that leveraged microservices. This approach not only lowered the unit's cost base but also offered more flexibility, enabled ecosystem partners to plug and play onto Domain's platform, and provided a motivational boost for development teams to experiment with partners and customers to create new solutions. Domain made some acquisitions, developed some ecosystem partnerships, and it was always on the lookout for new ecosystem partners. Over about seven years, Domain was transformed from a classified ads subsidiary to a go-to destination for the home customer domain for nearly 10 million customers.

What Leaders Should Focus On

Successfully leading a transformation along pathway 4 is all about getting the balance right. You need the fervor and drive of a startup, offering a solution to customers often focused on a customer domain rather than a traditional industry. This is typically a disruptive play, creating an offering quickly and getting customer acceptance, then developing the solution over time and bringing in partners for complementary products and services. The parent firm typically has constraints to produce business cases, adhere to governance requirements, and navigate the many layers of approvals and coordination that slow things down. Then again, there are many benefits to being owned by a larger company, such as access to customers, data, resources, and services like HR and technology.

To be successful on this pathway, leaders need to manage three of the explosions from day one: new ways of working, organizational surgery/redesign, and clarifying decision rights (see figure 6-4). And then, they must learn from the technology ecosystem winners and develop a platform mindset. The platforms won't be perfect and will need to be redone, but it's the platform mindset that makes a big difference. Very often in successful pathway 4 transformations, firms have looked beyond their current leadership to tap the CEO of the new unit. You need someone who has built this type of business before and is hungry to do it again and will develop a new, born future-ready, culture. The connection to the parent firm can be made through other members of the management team.

In pathway 4 initiatives, it is also important to think early on about how to capture value from the three sources: operations, customers, and ecosystems. The need to capture value from

6-4 Pathway 4—What Leaders Should Focus On

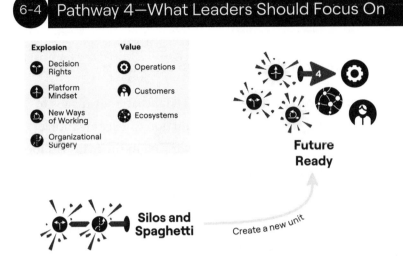

Source: The posited order of the actions results from our qualitative research. We tested our hypothesis that decision rights was the explosion to anticipate and manage first using hierarchical regression equations and the data from the MIT CISR 2019 Top Management Teams and Transformation Survey (N = 1,311).

multiple sources simultaneously, as well as the ability to do so, is one of the big differences between the newer, more digital units and established firms. Dashboarding is especially important in pathway 4, as there will be lots of course corrections in terms of creating and capturing value, and the team is typically small enough to be able to make those shifts relatively quickly.

In this chapter, as well as in the previous three chapters, we have discussed how to lead transformations on each of the four pathways toward future ready. In chapter 7, we will focus on the leadership issues needed for successful digitally enabled transformation across all pathways, including engaging the board and the top leadership team and discussing how to coordinate and manage multiple pathways.

Action Items from Chapter 6

The first three actions are common to every transformation.

1. Communicate today (and every day) that your firm is focusing on a pathway 4 transformation to become future ready. Paint a picture of what working in the firm will look like in the future, and articulate the steps along the way to help people understand their roles.

2. Collect stories of early success and distribute them widely—internally and externally. It's those early indicators of success that help keep motivation high, drive commitment and progress, and stem the impact of the doubters.

3. Create a plan for managing the explosions.

4. Identify your typical customer's end-to-end journey, considering how you could reduce friction for the customer—or even own a one-stop destination for your customers, as we saw in both TradeLens and Domain.

5. As part of your firm's communication plan about proceeding on pathway 4, highlight the particular problem the new unit will solve for customers and what changes in work and technology it will take to create the solution.

6. Decide on the leadership of the new unit—you may have to look outside the firm to get the startup expertise needed to create a new unit.

7. Digitally partner to reduce time to market and help grow revenues faster.[31]

8. Be prepared to adjudicate conflicts between the new unit and the existing firm. The investment in the new unit may be higher than in the existing firm, and it will be working in new ways with future-ready systems. There could be friction between employees and units.

9. Work on your exit strategy for the pathway 4 unit.

10. Identify and track metrics about ecosystem value accumulation.

11. Review the approaches taken by TradeLens and Domain to identify good ideas that can be adjusted to align with your firm's culture.

Chapter 7

Leading the Transformation

This book is all about becoming future ready. Future-ready firms are adaptable and able to succeed in almost any environment, and they outperform competitors on both growth and margin. Top performance comes from following one or more of the four pathways and building ten future-ready capabilities—which you have encountered in the cases, and we will summarize in this chapter. Plus, future-ready firms will have accumulated all three types of value along the way—value from customers, value from operations, and value from ecosystems. In this final chapter, we focus on the role of leadership in making the firm future ready. Leaders have to set the purpose, communicate the message, and give all the stakeholders—employees, customers, investors, regulators, and everyone else—confidence that the firm will make it and that everyone will prosper. That confidence is the essence of any successful transformation.

Top Management Teams

First, let's talk about the common language and understanding top management teams need to develop to successfully compete in the digital economy. There's little doubt that the future of business is digital. Having a top management team (TMT) that understands the role of digital in the firm's success makes a huge difference. Our MIT CISR research shows that large firms whose executive teams have that understanding—which we call digital savvy— outperformed other firms by more than 48 percent based on revenue growth and valuation.[1] And firms whose TMTs were in the top quartile of digital savvy were significantly further along in their transformation (69 percent complete) compared to firms with TMTs in the bottom quartile (30 percent complete). Once the TMT has begun to develop their digital savvy, they need to commit their time. A successful digital transformation is going to require perseverance from the entire TMT (as well as the entire firm). For example, the TMTs of firms that have made it to the final quartile of percent complete on their transformation spend 60 percent of their time on the transformation, which is a huge commitment. As Jean-Pascal Tricoire, chairman and CEO of Schneider Electric, a firm offering energy management and industrial automation, told us, "When every business becomes a digital business, every executive needs to take digital transformation personally. The last thing you want in your team is the belief that digital is somebody else's problem."[2]

We propose several TMT action items for all firms that want to succeed in their transformations and be top performers in the digital era:

1. Have a frank conversation about what percentage of your TMT are digitally savvy.[3] This is a great opportunity for

the CEO, head of HR, and the CIO to collaborate to educate the TMT.

2. Make the digital transformation the top commitment of the TMT—and support that commitment by investing time and allocating resources to the chosen pathway. Make sure the TMT communicates and models the commitment to the rest of the firm.

3. Involve the rest of the firm on this exciting digital journey. Provide them with opportunities for education, working in new areas and new collaborations, and be prepared to share success stories and lessons learned from what has worked well.

The Role of the Board

The board plays a pivotal role in digitally transforming the firm successfully. Board members tend to be older, more experienced, and less likely to be digital natives. But they are often fast learners and understand the need to get up to speed on the risks and opportunities of digital. The board will not be leading the transformation, but the most adept boards are an integral part of a transformation, encouraging change, asking pointed questions of the TMT, and providing encouragement, resources, and oversight. Now we will summarize what we have learned about the role of the board in a successful transformation.[4]

Assessing the Risk of Not Pursuing an Opportunity versus the Risk of Change

Digital changes everything—and having board members with experience in digital business is a new financial performance differentiator. But most boards do not have that experience. So how can executives and board chairs help their boards develop in this area?

A board needs to help oversee and guide the firm on its transformation to become future ready. A board needs to understand when the firm should commit to a course of action, experiment among alternatives, and partner to gain access to key resources and knowledge, and they should know the early indications of both success and challenges with digitally enabled initiatives operating at firm scale. These skills are critical for boards in perhaps their most important role in digital—asking the right questions of the management team as they propose and execute a transformation.

A board cannot rely on a single board member to have this understanding. We found that only firms with three or more board members with this sort of understanding of digital had superior performance.

To help boards manage discussion and agendas around digital and transformations, we developed a framework on the key areas a board must address—strategy, oversight, and defense:

- **Strategy**—identifying opportunities and threats to the firm's business model from digital and how the firm will succeed in the future

- **Oversight**—ensuring that the major digital transformations, projects, and technology spending are sensible and on track

- **Defense**—protecting the firm from cyber and other risks, as well as system outages, and ensuring data privacy and compliance

To effectively address each of the areas, boards, or more typically their chairs, must design board agendas and board member engagement to provide the time and resources needed.

Principal Financial Group: Creating a Digital Focus in the Boardroom

Principal Financial Group helps people, businesses, and institutions around the world "have enough, save enough, and protect enough" for their financial future through retirement, insurance, and asset management solutions. Principal has more than 34 million customers and $807 billion in assets under management.[5]

Digital business strategies became a routine topic for the Principal board almost a decade ago. The CEO and board tasked the CIO with leading corporate strategy to drive technology enablement further into the firm's business strategy.

Helping a board to become adept around digital (and thus able to understand the issues and do the necessary oversight of a transformation) requires a combination of agenda setting, common language, education, working the problem, and formal structures.

AGENDA SETTING AND COMMON LANGUAGE

Since the Principal board began pursuing digital business strategies, its agendas have included topics on technology, featuring presentations and discussions on strategy, oversight, and defense. Principal's (now former) CIO Gary Scholten estimated that just over 50 percent of the technology-related topics map to the area of strategy, with around 15 percent mapping to oversight and 35 percent to defense.

Strategy-oriented topics have covered business strategy implications of technology and technology-focused demos, education of board members, and funding. Oversight topics have included reviewing budget allocations and the progress of transformation projects. Defense topics have incorporated cybersecurity updates, including metrics, monitoring, and trends.

With more than 50 percent of its technology-related agenda spent on strategic issues, the focus of the Principal board has been clear—how digital can help Principal perform even better in the next decade. Aligning on a common framework and language for discussing and prioritizing digital strategies is critical in preventing board members from talking past one another.

Principal has adopted, used, and reused a handful of key frameworks that make discussions much more productive and efficient. The framework used is less important than picking one that makes sense to the firm and that will be reused, becoming the basis for decision-making and follow-up.

EDUCATION AND WORKING THE PROBLEM

Educating board and executive committee members on digital in a way that is engaging and nonthreatening is key. In addition to bringing those with less digital experience up to a foundational level, education helps to shift the members toward more common mental models on how to apply digital capabilities to the business and oversee any transformation.

Principal has leveraged external experts, fintech entrepreneurs, and internal technology and data experts in educational sessions. The CEO and CIO have organized executive committee digital immersion trips to help facilitate a common understanding of how digitally native firms compete. In addition to the value created as the executive committee debated its digital strategies, subsequent debriefings with the board have resulted in it gaining confidence that the executive team is better prepared to deal with the dramatic changes coming to their industry from digital transformation.

FORMAL STRUCTURES AND DECISION-MAKING

In 2015, Principal formed a digital strategy committee composed of business executives, their corresponding divisional CIOs, and the CMO, and chaired by the firm CIO. This committee was responsible for creating a common framework to develop digital business strategies, and it determines where to focus the application of strategies to business divisions versus the firm.

As we move rapidly into the digital era, boards have to adapt their important contribution to the firm. Boards are contributing to the success of digital business transformations by supporting the top management team, pushing the firm to consider the business models' risks of passivity, and overseeing the progress of the transformation. Many existing board members do not come from a digital background, but most we've met are very motivated to learn and change. Helping these board members is the responsibility not only of the chair and CEO but also of every member of the firm—and it pays off.

What Leaders Must Get Right

Once TMTs have a deep understanding of the competitive opportunities digital creates and a shared commitment to devote the time to the transformation, they can begin. To help leaders prioritize on this journey to future ready, we summarized what they must get right in chapter 1 (see figure 7-1). In chapters 2 through 6, we described the four pathways and the explosions. In this chapter, we'll concentrate on the creation and capture of value and the role of leadership.

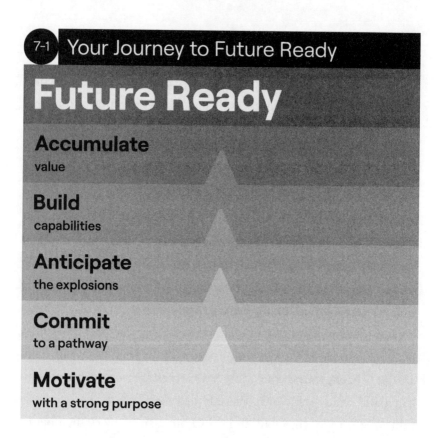

7-1 Your Journey to Future Ready

Future Ready

Accumulate
value

Build
capabilities

Anticipate
the explosions

Commit
to a pathway

Motivate
with a strong purpose

Here are the actions leaders must take to ensure the journey to future ready is successful:

- Motivate with a strong purpose.

- Commit to a pathway (or pathways).

- Anticipate the explosions.

- Build capabilities.

- Accumulate value.

Let's dive into each action.

Motivate with a Strong Purpose

To be meaningful and resonate with stakeholders, the firm's purpose has to be the driver of any transformation. The purpose not only guides the customization of your firm's version of future ready, but it also helps your people make judgments and trade-offs along the way. Do the decisions being made help meet the purpose? This is a great question for leaders to ask, particularly in times of uncertainty. Here are some firms' purposes that we admire:

- **Standard Bank Group** (the largest bank in Africa): "Africa is our home and we drive her growth."[6] This purpose unites the bank employees from twenty countries in Africa. Those employees are often asked in workshops and other settings how the decision they were discussing helped deliver on their purpose. This purpose contributed to Standard Bank's current vision to both "bank the ecosystem" and "be the ecosystem driver" in target areas, including health, trade, traders, home, and education.

- **Cochlear** (the global leader in implantable hearing solutions): "We help people hear and be heard."[7] Cochlear's drive to create new value, including enhancing the direct-to-wearer relationship and serving the ecosystem of candidates, wearers, clinicians, referrers, and players, was guided by this purpose.

- **Schneider Electric** (an energy and automation digital solution firm focusing on sustainability and efficiency): "Empower all to make the most of our energy and resources," dubbed "Life Is On."[8] This purpose has helped drive new business models based on electrification sustainability and digitization efficiency, helping Schneider to be ranked as the world's most sustainable corporation in 2021.[9]

- **Tetra Pak** (a global food processing and packaging solutions firm): "We commit to making food safe and available, everywhere."[10] This purpose has helped drive Tetra Pak's transformation, first by focusing on creating value from operations, then customers, and, more recently, ecosystems.

- **DBS** (the Singapore-based bank operating in Asia): "Making Banking Joyful."[11] This purpose motivated DBS's transformation to be the "world's leading bank" and going from last to first in customer experience in a span of about ten years.

- **TradeLens** (a Maersk business developing a global shipping platform): "Digitizing the global supply chain."[12] This purpose has propelled TradeLens to improve the experience of trade for all parties by better sharing of information, increasing transparency, and simplifying and automating processes.

- **Principal Financial Group** (a US financial services firm providing retirement, insurance, and asset management solutions): "To give you the financial tools, resources and information you need to live your best life."[13] This purpose guided Principal's efforts in embedding digital into their strategies to help people, businesses, and institutions manage their financial assets.

- **CarMax** (the largest US retailer of used cars and a disruptor in the automotive industry): "To drive integrity by being honest and transparent in every interaction."[14] This purpose underlies all of CarMax's endeavors in transforming the experience of buying a used car.

In your firm, do you have a similarly compelling purpose that helps guide decisions?

Commit to a Pathway

To move toward future ready from silos and spaghetti, every firm has to choose its pathway(s). Not being explicit about which pathway you are following leads to very frustrating outcomes. One of the most memorable workshops we conducted was with a large, publicly listed firm. We shared the framework with the CEO and the top management team of twelve people. We asked all of the participants to identify which pathways they were on and approximately how far along they were toward completion. As soon as the polling data appeared on the screen, there was an audible groan from the participants. Among the thirteen participants, there were seven different answers! Participants named just about every combination of pathways as the approach the firm was following—with lots of variation in percent complete. What followed was a very helpful but robust conversation about how different parts of the business were pursuing different pathways that were not coordinated. In the next polling question, we asked which pathway(s) the firm should follow, and the results were much more consistent. Not everyone had the same answer, but the results were more focused. After some more discussion, there was agreement that the firm should follow pathway 3, adding a pathway 4 ecosystem play operating as a separate unit.

To reinforce this point about choosing and committing to a pathway, let's review the results we discussed in chapter 2, figure 2-2. Firms that picked multiple pathways that were well-coordinated were, on average, 59 percent complete on their transformation compared to what was proposed to their boards. But firms on multiple pathways that were not coordinated were only 30 percent complete. And it's easy to see why. Firms on uncoordinated multiple pathways are working at cross purposes, always reinventing the wheel and not learning effectively from one another or reusing the capabilities they have built. Plus, most importantly, they are often confusing their customer with multiple (unintegrated) offers and making it difficult for their employees to support all this complexity. It's not easy to get agreement on the pathways, and choosing multiple pathways for a transformation makes managing the transformation even more challenging.

If your firm needs to commit to a transformation involving multiple pathways, think back to the case studies we describe in the book. Which appeal to you? Revisit what they did to see what you can learn from them.

Anticipate Explosions

One of the most common questions we are asked is how to change the culture so it will support the transformation to future ready. There is a lot of great (and not so great) literature on culture change, and as students of organizations, we have enjoyed reading it. But when we collaborate with firms as they think about their cultures, our advice is pragmatic. Don't explicitly try and change the culture—that is a multilayered, political, long-term, and complicated endeavor. Getting agreement on the description of the as-is culture and then designing the to-be culture is a great activity for the TMT, but changing the culture is difficult to do as a stand-alone objective. Instead, we recommend that you focus on managing the four explosions. Changing the culture happens when people change the way they think and the way they work—changing their habits. If you manage the four explosions effectively, you will change the culture in the areas targeted for transformation. And that culture change will reinforce your transformation.

Here is a quick summary of the four explosions. As you read, start thinking about how well you are managing the explosions today. In chapter 2, we provided an assessment and benchmarks so you can see how effectively you manage the explosions.

- **Decision rights:** This explosion is about getting the right people to lead key decisions. Some of the key decisions include clarifying who decides what to do and who decides how to do it, prioritizing the spending for digital investments, determining which group(s) in the firm can make new digital offers to customers, and agreeing on the decisions that can be made by teams doing the work (e.g., this involves assessing the level of risk your firm is comfortable with your teams taking on).

- **New ways of working:** Digital enables new ways of working, like agile methodologies, evidence-based decision-making, and creating minimal viable products that are offered to customers in a test-and-learn way. New ways of working change collective work habits and help transform the culture.

- **Platform mindset:** A firm with a platform mindset creates and reuses platforms that take their crown jewels and turn them into digital services, connect organizational silos, share data, and standardize processes.

- **Organizational surgery:** There is a time in most transformations when the leaders realize that the way they are organized is not optimal for the firm's aspirations. At this point, the firm typically does some kind of organizational surgery, often to integrate silos and increase collaboration across the firm to achieve better customer experience and more efficient operations.

We suggest you review the case studies of Tetra Pak, CEMEX, KPN, and Domain in chapters 3 through 6. You will find some great ideas on how to manage the explosions and some motivating details on what they got right.

Build Capabilities

An important and far-reaching aspiration is to build ten future-ready capabilities across the entire firm, including the board, top management team, and everyone else. These capabilities help a firm become future ready and then help sustain competitive advantage. This is not a one-and-done initiative but an ongoing effort that requires leadership, purpose, goal, metrics, budget, fresh approaches, and perseverance.

In chapter 1, we introduced the future-ready capabilities. These are the capabilities that make transformation happen and enable you to accumulate new digital value. We think of these capabilities as HOW your firm will create value. Focusing on building these ten capabilities is the best and most succinct recipe we know for moving a firm toward future ready and increasing financial performance.[15] We have organized the ten capabilities by the types of digital value they are most important for, as well as the four capabilities that are foundational and common to all types of value.

Future-Ready Capabilities to Create Value from Operations

BECOME MODULAR, OPEN, AND AGILE

A future-ready firm creates modular digitized services to both optimize operations and design and create new offerings. To continually innovate at low cost, firms have to take what makes them great—their crown jewels—and turn them into modular, digitized services. These services can then be combined and recombined, like LEGO blocks, into many different digital offerings, sold and delivered both through their direct channels and via partners.

STRIVE FOR AMBIDEXTERITY

To be successful for decades to come, firms have to innovate to engage and delight customers while simultaneously reducing costs by means of readily available technologies—for example, cloud computing or application programming interfaces (APIs), often combined with agile test-and-learn approaches. With one hand, firms relentlessly reduce costs every year. With the other hand, they constantly innovate, finding new and better ways to do everything. Future-ready firms create a rhythm of removing costs and innovating, setting them up for being top performers.

Future-Ready Capabilities to Create Value from Customers

PROVIDE A GREAT MULTIPRODUCT CUSTOMER EXPERIENCE

To continually delight customers, future-ready firms integrate their many products into a seamless multiproduct, often a multichannel customer experience, which reflects a typical customer journey. Customers get a great experience no matter which channel they choose, and the firm strives to meet customers' needs rather than push products. This requires removing or at least hiding the silos of products or geography that exist in many firms.

BE PURPOSE-DRIVEN

Increasingly, leaders, customers, employees, investors, and partners are demanding that firms have a strong purpose for existence beyond the maximization of shareholder wealth. We saw an example of this power with Standard Bank Group's "Africa is our home, we drive her growth," being a unifying purpose both inside and outside the bank. Creating a firm purpose that brings people together provides a worthy reason for being and encourages excellence is a wonderful North Star for any successful journey to future ready.

Future-Ready Capabilities to Create Value from Ecosystems

LEAD OR PARTICIPATE IN ECOSYSTEMS

Future-ready firms are ecosystem-ready—whether they lead or participate in an ecosystem or both—and work digitally with a wide variety of partners. The firms that lead ecosystems—we call them ecosystem drivers—create go-to destinations for their customers and partner with other firms providing a broad range of curated products. The firms that participate in ecosystems—we call them modular producers—provide digitized products that easily plug and play into those ecosystems. We found that firms operating in ecosystems grew faster and were more profitable.[16]

PURSUE DYNAMIC (AND DIGITAL) PARTNERSHIPS

In the digital era, the fastest-growing firms digitally partner to increase both reach and range. They partner with some firms to reach new customers, and they partner with other firms to broaden the range of products they offer to their current customers. This partnering is not the traditional strategic, exclusive partnering that is built on tightly integrated processes. Instead, much of digital partnering is automated and seamless via APIs, usually based on computer-to-computer sharing of data, transactions, and insights.[17] Amazon, PayPal, and Climate are masters at digital partnering to help fuel their growth.

Future-Ready Foundational Capabilities for Creating Value

TREAT DATA AS A STRATEGIC ASSET

We have opined for years about data becoming a strategic asset—a single source of truth, supported by an ethical set of data monetization capabilities, accessible and used to make evidence-based decisions. Future-ready firms get closer to this nirvana by continuously standardizing, cleaning, simplifying, and learning how to monetize their data by improving internal processes, improving products by wrapping data for new features and experiences, and/or selling data.[18]

DEVELOP AND RETAIN THE RIGHT TALENT

Transforming a workforce to future ready requires leaders to both equip people with the technologies they need and give them the accountability and capabilities (i.e., skills and collaborative culture) to fully exploit those tools. As firms adopt agile methods, data analytics, robotics, AI, and other digital technologies and approaches, what they demand of their employees is changing. While ensuring that employees have the right skills for their roles is important, it is just as important to empower their workforce to work collaboratively to solve complex problems.[19] BBVA, a global financial group headquartered in Madrid, is an example of a firm explicitly tying developing and retaining talent to their future-ready goals. In February 2014, BBVA established a subsidiary called BBVA Data & Analytics (D&A). BBVA leaders quickly realized that D&A's techniques and analytics could (1) generate large financial value via internal improvements to operations and (2) be used to create meaningful new features and customer experiences for their digital products—key to bank transformation efforts. BBVA's strategy to cultivate contemporary data science talent combined recruitment, internal development programs, and retooling efforts.[20]

LINK INDIVIDUAL AND TEAM BEHAVIORS TO FIRM GOALS

One of the distinctive characteristics of future-ready firms is that they have moved from a command-and-control to a coach-and-communicate leadership style, guiding employees with accountability rather than telling them what to do. An explicit linking of individual and team behaviors to firm goals also helps employees in their decision-making. Many firms like DBS achieve this by linking through dashboards with new key performance indicators (KPIs) and incentive models. DBS reduced the focus on traditional KPIs (like sustainable growth and bank of choice) in the group scorecard, adding 20 percent on "making banking joyful" for customers and employees. One of the KPIs was income per digital customer, and the group scorecard gave each employee guidance on how they could contribute.[21]

FACILITATE RAPID LEARNING THROUGHOUT THE FIRM

Given that the future is, by definition, uncertain, being future ready requires rapidly learning and adapting. Learning from born-digital firms, existing firms are adopting more digital ways of working, including setting up multifunctional agile teams, using test-and-learn approaches, relying on evidence-based decision-making, and building platforms rather than silos and spaghetti. Using new iterative ways of working, future-ready firms mindfully explore ideas, develop opportunities to identify value, work to create value, and then scale the learnings throughout the firm.[22] They create new value by combining rapid learning with traditional strengths like having a large customer base, amazing data, and people who know the industry and the key business processes.

The differences in the effectiveness of the ten capabilities between firms that are in silos and spaghetti (i.e., firms wrestling with a complex landscape of technology, processes, and data and that are typically product-driven rather than customer-focused) and firms that have made the journey to future ready are stark (see figure 7-2). As your firm moves along on its transformation pathway(s), keep in mind the need to build and strengthen these capabilities. They are key to helping your firm capture value. Why not start now? Run your eye down the items in figure 7-2 and identify your firm's strengths and weaknesses and perhaps pick the top three to focus on.

Accumulate Value

We have now addressed all components of figure 7-1 except accumulating and tracking value. We think of accumulating value as the WHAT of a digital transformation. In this book, we have

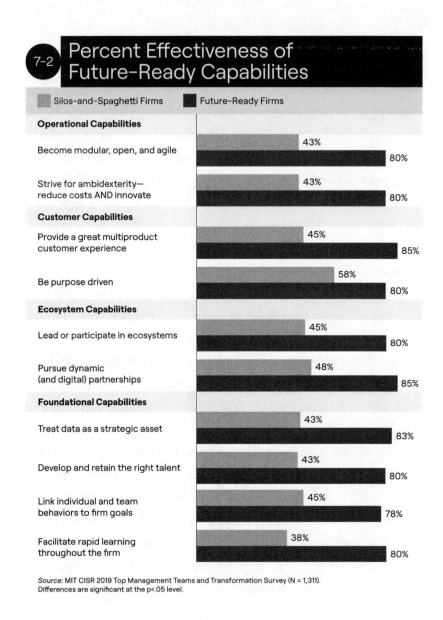

7-2 Percent Effectiveness of Future-Ready Capabilities

Silos-and-Spaghetti Firms   Future-Ready Firms

Operational Capabilities

Become modular, open, and agile — 43% / 80%

Strive for ambidexterity— reduce costs AND innovate — 43% / 80%

Customer Capabilities

Provide a great multiproduct customer experience — 45% / 85%

Be purpose driven — 58% / 80%

Ecosystem Capabilities

Lead or participate in ecosystems — 45% / 80%

Pursue dynamic (and digital) partnerships — 48% / 85%

Foundational Capabilities

Treat data as a strategic asset — 43% / 83%

Develop and retain the right talent — 43% / 80%

Link individual and team behaviors to firm goals — 45% / 78%

Facilitate rapid learning throughout the firm — 38% / 80%

Source: MIT CISR 2019 Top Management Teams and Transformation Survey (N = 1,311). Differences are significant at the p<.05 level.

described three types of value that firms capture as part of their transformation:[23]

- Value from operations—this value comes from increasing efficiency, reducing costs, and increasing speed and reuse.

- Value from customers—this value comes from delighting customers and is reflected in generating more revenue per customer, including more revenue from new offerings, and increasing customer stickiness.

- Value from ecosystems—your firm gets this value as it increases its revenue from ecosystems, its revenue from partners, and collects more data from the ecosystem.

As firms progress along their pathway to future ready, they capture all three types of value.

What to Focus on First

One of the most important tasks when transforming your firm to becoming future ready is accumulating and tracking value over time. To get started, we have identified what leaders have to focus on first in each of the four pathways regarding value creation and the four explosions (see figure 7-3 for a listing of which explosion and which type of value to focus on first, by pathway). Focus is so important when there are many moving parts.

On all pathways, the first explosion to focus on is decision rights—identifying who can make the key decisions and then holding those people accountable. Changing the decision rights for a handful of key decisions, like who decides how technology dollars are spent, sets up the firm to move along its chosen pathway.

For pathway 1, the focus on decision rights is followed by creating a platform mindset. Value from operations is the first value focus on pathway 1. For pathway 2, after decision rights, new ways of working is the next most important explosion to focus on. Value from customers is the first value focus. For pathway 3,

7-3 Initial Focus(es) on Each Pathway			
Pathway	**Explosion**		**Value**
Pathway 1	⚙ Decision Rights	✈ Platform Mindset	◎ Operations
Pathway 2	⚙ Decision Rights	🖲 New Ways of Working	🧑 Customers
Pathway 3	⚙ Decision Rights		🧑 Customers ◎ Operations
Pathway 4	⚙ Decision Rights	🩹 Organizational Surgery	🌐 Ecosystems

Source: The posited order of the actions results from our qualitative research. We tested our hypothesis that decision rights was the explosion to anticipate and manage first using hierarchical regression equations and the data from the MIT CISR 2019 Top Management Teams and Transformation Survey (N = 1,311).

allocating decision rights is even more important. Moving back and forth between customer experience and operational efficiency puts a real strain on decision rights, and it's the most important explosion to get right and adjust over time. As you move up the stair steps on pathway 3, creating new value from customers and value from operations is equally important early on. For pathway 4, the most important explosion after decision rights is organizational surgery because you are designing a born-digital organization that doesn't rely on existing organizational silos and can operate with high agility. One of the most important decisions is deciding what to use and not to use from the parent firm. Of course, value from operations and customers is important, but the first value focus for most pathway 4 units is typically to create value from ecosystems—in particular, partnering with other firms to seamlessly bring in customers and complementary products and services.

Dashboard Your Transformation

In an activity as uncertain as digitally transforming a large organization, knowing where you are is as important as knowing where you want to go. To know where you are requires two important types of value measures: (1) effectiveness at building capabilities future-ready companies must have to thrive in the digital era (the HOW) and (2) indicators of transformation success (the WHAT), such as progress and value capture. The most effective tool we have seen companies use to know where they are is real-time dashboarding.

In our analysis of over one thousand companies, those that were more effective at dashboarding were also better at most other important measures, including innovation, growth, and margin relative to industry (see figure 7-4). The results speak for themselves and emphasize why we are finishing the book by focusing on dashboarding. There are lots of reasons why dashboarding is so effective, but perhaps the most important is that everybody gets to see how the firm is doing against agreed-upon metrics, working together to make course corrections when necessary.

We propose that an effective dashboard monitors two aspects of value from digital:

- WHAT value is captured, tracking this over time.

- HOW value is created via the development of organizational and individual future-ready capabilities.

The combination of the *what* and *how* of creating value from digital drives the company toward becoming future ready. Schneider Electric tracks these aspects in a dashboard the company created that it calls the Digital Flywheel.

7-4 Firms That Are Highly Effective at Dashboarding Outperform

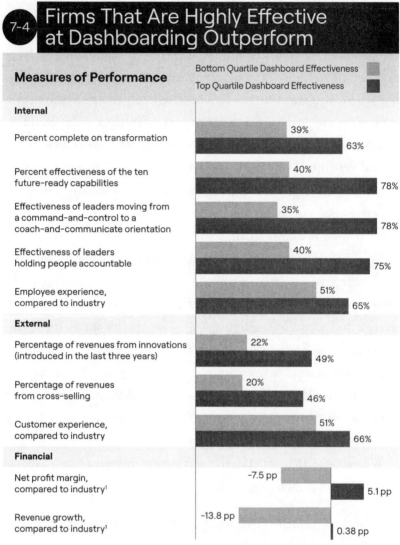

Measures of Performance

Bottom Quartile Dashboard Effectiveness

Top Quartile Dashboard Effectiveness

Internal

Percent complete on transformation
- 39%
- 63%

Percent effectiveness of the ten future-ready capabilities
- 40%
- 78%

Effectiveness of leaders moving from a command-and-control to a coach-and-communicate orientation
- 35%
- 78%

Effectiveness of leaders holding people accountable
- 40%
- 75%

Employee experience, compared to industry
- 51%
- 65%

External

Percentage of revenues from innovations (introduced in the last three years)
- 22%
- 49%

Percentage of revenues from cross-selling
- 20%
- 46%

Customer experience, compared to industry
- 51%
- 66%

Financial

Net profit margin, compared to industry[1]
- -7.5 pp
- 5.1 pp

Revenue growth, compared to industry[1]
- -13.8 pp
- 0.38 pp

[1] Self-reported net profit margin/revenue growth correlates significantly with actual profit margin/revenue growth at the p<.01 level. Net profit margin and revenue growth are compared to industry and are 5% mean trimmed to remove outliers.
Source: MIT CISR 2019 Top Management Teams and Transformation Survey (N = 1,311).

Schneider Electric Tracks Value Creation with Its Digital Flywheel

Schneider Electric SE is a €28.9 billion revenue company providing digital solutions for energy management and industrial automation.[24] Over the last decade, Schneider Electric has transformed itself from a seller of energy-related products to a digital leader in providing energy-efficiency services.

For Schneider Electric and its customers, the combination of the sustainability of electrification and the efficiency gains that digitization supports offers great new value creation potential. To implement this strategy, Schneider created EcoStruxure, an Internet-of-Things-enabled plug-and-play customer engagement system delivering energy efficiency as a service for use in buildings, factories, data centers, and so on. The EcoStruxure system translates data into actionable intelligence by collecting structured (from sensors) and unstructured (from logs completed by maintenance people) data from the set of Schneider Electric products at a customer site and analyzing the data. This produces a set of real-time instructions that the system sends back to the customer site. EcoStruxure and other capabilities have enabled Schneider Electric to move from selling products to selling more services and software. These digital solutions can make a big difference in customer sites. For example, companies using Schneider Electric's energy efficiency solutions report a 30 percent reduction in energy consumption.

Achieving this kind of transformation in a large organization requires a way for everyone to understand the organization's goals, metrics, and business logic and how they fit together. For Schneider Electric, the Digital Flywheel provided such guidance, becoming a tool to help drive the transformation.

Schneider Electric first represented its dashboard as a "digital barometer" that measured *what* value was created from digital. But soon, senior leaders realized that something additional was needed—the business logic of *how* value, including sales, was to be created—to help internal and external stakeholders understand why particular metrics were important. This led to the creation of the Digital Flywheel, which describes and tracks how value is created via digital. The Digital Flywheel has four key components, representing the four parts of the EcoStruxure system:

- **Connectable Products:** all the energy-related systems and devices in a building, including heating and cooling systems, ventilation, and thermostats. These products supply data for analysis and receive and act on instructions.

- **Edge Control:** a software and monitoring solutions layer that gives organizations the ability to coordinate and manage the connectable products.

- **Digital and Software:** a layer of intelligence and software that performs analytics and generates energy efficiency dashboards in real time. Besides connectable Schneider products, the software can also manage competitor and complementary physical products. Analyses of product-generated data identify additional needs and opportunities.

- **Field Services:** teams that implement Schneider products and services.

On the Digital Flywheel, Schneider Electric captures and tracks financial performance both for the four components individually and combined. But just as important is that it shows how the four components work together to produce higher value and sales for the company—and increased value for clients, often measured as energy efficiency improvement. Total firm revenues generated via EcoStruxure have grown from a very small percentage following its debut in 2016 to 50 percent in 2021[25]—an industry-leading achievement and a tangible illustration of Schneider

Electric's shift from mostly product sales to selling both products and services.[26]

Dashboard Effectively by Applying Five Lessons

Schneider Electric's use of the Digital Flywheel has changed how the company is managed. We examined the company's development and use of the Flywheel and surfaced five lessons:

1. **Combine both what and how.** In creating the Digital Flywheel, it took Schneider Electric many rounds of iteration to arrive at the effective version. What makes the Digital Flywheel compelling is how it combines *what* the company should measure with the business logic of *how* the value is created.

2. **Persist.** It takes time to get an organization to adopt and use a dashboard. Schneider Electric, like most companies that successfully use dashboards, went through phases where people resisted using it. Eventually, company executives reached an agreement on common definitions and metrics for the drivers of business success. Once such agreement is reached, people can use a dashboard as a team tool to understand how their group operates and connects to the performance of other groups.

3. **Use the dashboard to manage the company.** At Schneider Electric, CEO Jean-Pascal Tricoire uses the Digital Flywheel in his quarterly reviews with each business leader. The conversations typically start with covering what has worked well and then moves to areas that need additional focus. The Digital Flywheel provides a common language

for use across the entire company—even by the board in their digital subcommittee. Recently, the Digital Flywheel was used in Schneider Electric's investor relations presentation to demonstrate how digital and services combine to create a compelling vision proposition.

4. **Communicate to the entire company how to use the dashboard.** Getting an entire large company to effectively use a dashboard requires wide-ranging, consistent communication. To reach its 135,000 employees, Schneider Electric used a variety of ways to broadcast the message. One successful approach was a monthly newsletter focused on the Digital Flywheel. A recent edition had a section titled "Behind the Data in the Flywheel," with an interview of a senior Schneider Electric executive explaining the different types of churn and what actions can minimize churn. The goal was not only to further the use of the Flywheel but also to improve the company's performance on the metrics.

5. **Automate with drill-down capabilities.** As the dashboard moves closer to sharing real-time data with added capabilities to drill down into business and operational segments, it will become more effective and useful in company decision-making and ease course correction moving forward. At Schneider Electric, much of the data is real-time, and the dashboard filter panel displays the source of the data being examined and options to drill down on geography, business scope, and more.

In dashboarding, like many other digital initiatives, seeking perfection is the enemy of progress. The data won't be perfect or even agreed-upon in the first few rounds of creating your dashboard. Even more challenging will be changing the firm habits to use a common dashboard rather than local numbers. Plus, changing how you do management reviews with real-time dashboards will take time and reinforcement. But perhaps the most challenging and important effort will be articulating the business logic that shows how value is created and captured by the company. Including that business logic in a dashboard demonstrates that the leadership really has invested sufficient time and experience in understanding how digital will create new value for the company. Companies that have been successful with dashboarding typically started using the tool to measure and course correct a digitally enabled business transformation, but it eventually becomes the way to run the business.

Build Your Dashboard

In this section, we introduce a dashboard starter kit. Our dashboard is designed to provide a reading for everyone in the firm to see how they're doing against their goals with benchmarks from other firms for comparison. There are three important parts to the dashboard:

- Tracking the three types of value created over time (WHAT value is created). Assessing this value could require investments and iterations to get meaningful results.

- Assessing your ten future-ready capabilities that drive value creation (HOW the value is created).

- Benchmarking your firm's results to the average firm at the same stage of transformation. Is your firm making adequate progress compared to other firms?

187

Creating the dashboard has four steps. We suggest that you get multiple people to provide data and average their responses for a score for the whole firm and also look at variation across the different parts of the firm. Be prepared—completing parts of this dashboard is a challenge. Assessing value (the WHAT) requires having a deep understanding of how your firm makes money.

1. Determine how far along your firm is on its transformation (figure 7-5a). We have provided benchmarks for three stages of a transformation.

2. Complete figure 7-5b to assess your effectiveness at creating the three types of value (the WHAT). You will have three scores: value from operations, value from customers, and value from ecosystems

3. Complete figure 7-5c to assess the effectiveness of your ten future-ready capabilities (the HOW) on a percentage scale. You will have four scores: operations capabilities, customer capabilities, ecosystem capabilities, and foundational capabilities.

4. Enter your scores on figure 7-6 in the appropriate column for percent complete, and compare your answers to our benchmarks from more than a thousand firms globally. Where do you need to focus relative to the benchmarks?[27] And can you articulate the business logic underlying the creation and capture of value?

Let's return to our BankCo example to work through an example of how to use the dashboard. The information for BankCo is drawn from senior executives' assessments of value and capabilities done

7-5 Transformation Dashboard Assessment

Use these scores to fill in the transformation dashboard (figure 7-6).

a Transformation Progress

How far along is your firm on its digital business transformation (i.e., percentage complete) based on what was proposed to the board or CEO (from chapter 2, figure 2-5)?

%

b WHAT Type of Value Does Your Firm Accumulate?

Value from Operations Score
(0% = significantly worse than competitors, 100% = significantly better than competitors)

How competitive is your firm's cost of operations? %

How competitive is your firm's operational efficiency? %   Average

How competitive is your firm's speed to market? %

%

Value from Customers Score

What percentage of your firm's revenues comes from cross-selling? %

What percentage of your firm's revenues comes from innovations introduced in the last three years? %   Average

How effective is your firm at creating customer stickiness? (0% = not effective, 100% = extremely effective) %

%

Value from Ecosystems Score

What percentage of your firm's revenues comes from participating in or leading ecosystems? %

How effective is your firm at generating revenues from new ecosystem offerings with partners? (0% = not effective, 100% = extremely effective) %   Average

What percentage of the data from the ecosystem does your firm have access to? %

%

(continued)

7-5 Transformation Dashboard Assessment

Use these scores to fill in the transformation dashboard (figure 7-6)

c HOW Does Your Firm Create Value?

On a scale from 0% (not effective) to 100% (extremely effective), estimate your firm's effectiveness at achieving the stated capabilities, then average each set of answers to get your % scores.

Operational Capabilities Score

Become modular, open, and agile	%
Strive for ambidexterity (innovating and cutting cost simultaneously)	%

Average   %

Customer Capabilities Score

Provide a great multiproduct customer experience	%
Be purpose driven	%

Average   %

Ecosystem Capabilities Score

Lead or participate in ecosystems	%
Pursue dynamic (and digital) partnerships	%

Average   %

Foundational Capabilities Score

Link individual and team behaviors to firm goals	%
Facilitate rapid learning throughout the firm	%
Treat data as a strategic asset (collecting, curating, and monetizing)	%
Develop and retain the right talent	%

Average   %

Source: Benchmarks calculated from the MIT CISR 2019 Top Management Teams and Transformation Survey (N = 1,311).

7-6 Your Firm's Transformation Dashboard

Percent Complete on Transformation	0–33%	34–67%	68–100%

Retrieve your firm's % complete from 7-5a on the transformation dashboard assessment. Insert it here in the matching column. Your firm's benchmarks are in that column.

Your score			

Percent Value Accumulated (from 7-5b)

Value from Operations Score

Your score			
Avg. score	40%	54%	66%

Value from Customers Score

Your score			
Avg. score	26%	43%	55%

Value from Ecosystems Score

Your score			
Avg. score	28%	43%	69%

Effectiveness of Future-Ready Capabilities (from 7-5c)

Operational Capabilities Score

Your score			
Avg. score	33%	59%	71%

Customer Capabilities Score

Your score			
Avg. score	48%	65%	75%

Ecosystem Capabilities Score

Your score			
Avg. score	40%	63%	74%

Foundational Capabilities Score

Your score			
Avg. score	38%	59%	71%

Source: Benchmarks calculated from the MIT CISR 2019 Top Management Teams and Transformation Survey (N = 1,311). Firms that have completed 0–33% of their transformation are 25% of sample and are on average 21% complete. Firms that have completed 34–67% of their transformation are 44% of sample and are on average 51% complete. Firms that have completed 68–100% of their transformation are 29% of sample and are on average 80% complete.

during a workshop, and it is consolidated onto the dashboard, using some research interpretation (see figure 7-7).

BankCo is 55 percent complete on its digital transformation using multiple pathways—pathway 1 (60 percent of investment), pathway 2 (30 percent of investment), and pathway 4 (10 percent of investment). It is below the benchmark for both value from operations and customers but well above the benchmark for value from ecosystems. The likely cause is that both investment and management attention is focused on the pathway 4 ecosystem play, which is going well. The problem is that the lag in both value from operations and value from customers will put stress on the pathway 1 and 2 transformation efforts—these are focused on the existing bank where the big impacts will be—and these efforts need immediate attention.

To better understand the issues BankCo faces, let's now look at the future-ready capability scores. The foundational capabilities category scores are well below the benchmark. These need attention, so BankCo must examine the four capabilities that make up the foundational category to see which ones are below the benchmark.[28] For BankCo, the problem items were strategic use of data and firmwide rapid learning. We would make the following recommendations for action:

- Celebrate the successes of the value created from ecosystems by sharing customer stories and case studies both internally and externally to help generate momentum.

- Use the momentum from the customer stories to apply energy to the value capture efforts on pathways 1 and 2. Drill into the metrics on these paths to understand where the

7-7 BankCo's Transformation Dashboard

Percent Complete on Transformation	0–33%	34–67%	68–100%

Retrieve your firm's % complete from 7-5a on the transformation dashboard assessment. Insert it here in the matching column. Your firm's benchmarks are in that column.

BankCo's score		55%	

Multiple pathways
Pathway 1 (60% focus)
Pathway 2 (30% focus)
Pathway 4 (10% focus)

Percent Value Accumulated (from 7-5b)

Value from Operations Score

BankCo's score		48%	
Avg. score	40%	54%	66%

Value from Customers Score

BankCo's score		37%	
Avg. score	26%	43%	55%

Value from Ecosystems Score

BankCo's score		60%	
Avg. score	28%	43%	69%

Effectiveness of Future-Ready Capabilities (from 7-5c)

Operational Capabilities Score

BankCo's score		75%	
Avg. score	33%	59%	71%

Customer Capabilities Score

BankCo's score		69%	
Avg. score	48%	65%	75%

Ecosystem Capabilities Score

BankCo's score		80%	
Avg. score	40%	63%	74%

Foundational Capabilities Score

BankCo's score		42%	
Avg. score	38%	59%	71%

Source: Percent complete is based on the average of responses from five senior executives and assessments of value and capabilities are based on research interpretation. Benchmarks calculated from the MIT CISR 2019 Top Management Teams and Transformation Survey (N = 1,311).

challenges are capturing value from operations and from customers.

- Investigate why the higher-than-benchmark levels of operations and customer future-ready capabilities are not translating into value capture. Is this an overly optimistic perception by the executives in the workshop, or does governance or reusing digital services and modules need tweaking to take more advantage of the higher-than-average capabilities?

- Address the low scores of foundational capabilities—strategic use of data and firmwide rapid learning. This is often a decision-rights and platform-mindset issue created by local decision rights and abetted by local technology solutions with no mechanism for sharing firm-wide.

We recommend that you do this assessment once every three months of your transformation and track the scores over time, holding a workshop to discuss. The individual percentages of each score are much less important than the quality of the conversation that the scores stimulate. Over time, we recommend that you replace the perceptual and actual measures we've provided with actual real-time data that is most relevant to your HOW and WHAT.

Is Being Future Ready Achievable?

We are now at the end of the book, and we wish you every success in your transformation toward future ready. It's an exciting and rewarding management journey, and we look forward to hearing more about your successes and lessons learned. One more important question remains: Is it really possible to become future ready? Our answer is simple—yes! But the problem is that you can only become future ready at a point in time. The ten future-ready capabilities are the underpinnings, but you must continue to evolve them. In many of the analyses we've done, we compare a firm to its competitors, as you have done in your self-assessments. And those competitors, like you, get better over time, so the bar continues to rise. We recommend that you set a target date for becoming future ready (relative to competitors) and assess your progress over time. But once you get to that target date, the end-point is likely to have changed, and you will need to repeat the process all over again with a new target date. And this process will continue . . . forever! We wish you every success in your journey to becoming future ready—again and again!

Action Items for Chapter 7

1. Review the action items from all of the previous chapters, as they lay out the key decisions that need to have been made at each point.

2. Start educating the board and the top management team to become more digitally savvy. Bring in outside experts, do technology demos, rely on your internal talent, and experiment with reverse mentoring.

3. The way you lead the firm will have to change, especially as people change the way they work. A command-and-control style is not going to cut it—there will be demands on leadership to do more coaching and more communicating.

4. Decide which future-ready capabilities to work on first.

5. Articulate to the entire firm the business logic of WHAT value the digital transformation will accumulate and HOW that value will be created. Your dashboard should depict that business logic and use real-time data (as the goal).

6. More than anything else, your role as a leader is to make the transformation meaningful to everyone in the firm and give them the confidence that they can do it. You must embed the firm's purpose in the firm's actions, tell stories that capture why the firm is transforming, and be a visible role model of how you want employees to change and act.

Notes

Chapter 1

1. Throughout this book, we will use "firm" to represent all enterprises. In our research, teaching, and workshops, we have found the framework to be broadly applicable to for-profit firms, not-for-profit organizations, and government.

2. See Sebastian, I. M., Weill, P., and Woerner, S. L., "Driving Growth in Digital Ecosystems," *MIT Sloan Management Review* (Fall 2020, Reprint 62127): https://sloanreview.mit.edu/article/driving-growth-in-digital-ecosystems/.

3. See Weill, P., Woerner, S. L., and Shah, A., "Does Your C-Suite Have Enough Digital Smarts?," *MIT Sloan Management Review* (Spring 2021, Reprint 62320): https://sloanreview.mit.edu/article/does-your-c-suite-have-enough-digital-smarts/. On December 15, 2020, Inspire Brands completed its acquisition of Dunkin' Brands. Dunkin' and Baskin-Robbins are now operated as distinct brands within the Inspire portfolio. https://www.dunkinbrands.com/firm/about/about-dunkin-brands.

4. Application programming interface (API) refers to a set of functions and procedures that allows the creation of applications that access the features or data of an operating system, service, or another application.

5. A number of MIT CISR research projects collectively serve as the basis for this book. They include MIT CISR research on pathways to digital transformation, business models, digital partnering, value creation and value capture, replatforming, and domains. In 2015, we surveyed 413 respondents (MIT CISR 2015 CIO Digital Disruption Survey) and had over fifty conversations with executives in 2016 about their goals for digital business transformation. The analyses and conversations helped us create the future-ready quadrants. In 2017, we did another survey to study the four pathways (MIT CISR 2017 Digital Pathways Survey [N=400]). We did four in-depth case

studies of firms in 2018 (Tetra Pak, CEMEX, KPN, and Domain) to examine their digital business transformation, including their pathway and the four explosions. At each company, we conducted semistructured interviews with one or more members of the executive team (typically the CIO or company equivalent) and a direct report, asking them to openly share their digital business transformation experiences. In 2019 we administered a survey (MIT CISR 2019 TMT and Transformation Survey) to 1,311 respondents from around the globe asking questions about the digital transformation journey, how the explosions were managed, and the leadership actions and business mechanisms that facilitated the transformation.

6. Mean of self-reported revenues after doing a 5 percent mean trim.

7. See Sia, S. K., Weill, P., and Zhang, N., "Designing a Future-Ready Enterprise: The Digital Transformation of DBS Bank," *California Management Review* (March 2021); Sia, S. K., Weill, P., and Xu, M., "DBS: From the 'World's Best Bank' to Building the Future-Ready Enterprise," Nanyang Business School, December 2018, Ref No.: ABCC-2019-001.

8. Ross, J. W., Sebastian, I. M., and Beath C.M., "Digital Design: It's a Journey," *MIT Sloan CISR Research Briefing* 26, no. 4 (April 2016): https://cisr.mit.edu/publication/2016_0401_DigitalDesign_RossSebastianBeath.

9. Weill, P., and Woerner, S. L., "Dashboarding Pays Off," *MIT Sloan CISR Research Briefing* 22 (January 1, 2022): https://cisr.mit.edu/publication/2022_0101_Dashboarding_WeillWoerner.

10. Weill, P., and Woerner, S. L., *What's Your Digital Business Model? Six Questions to Help You Build the Next-Generation Enterprise* (Boston: Harvard Business Review Press, 2018).

11. Sebastian, I. M., Weill, P., and Woerner, S. L., "Three Strategies to Grow via Digital Partnering," *MIT Sloan CISR Research Briefing* 20, no. 5 (May 2020): https://cisr.mit.edu/publication/2020_0501_DigitalPartnering Strategies_SebastianWeillWoerner.

12. Modular producers are firms that provide plug-and-play services that adapt to a variety of ecosystems. These businesses are typically based on digital platforms with a set of API-enabled services and are technology agnostic. For more details, see Weill and Woerner, *What's Your Digital Business Model?*

Chapter 2

1. Weill, P., Woerner, S. L., and Harte, M., "Replatforming the Enterprise," *MIT Sloan Center for Information Systems Research Briefing* 20, no. 7 (July 2020): https://cisr.mit.edu/publication/2020_0701_Replatforming_WeillWoernerHarte.

Notes

2. Ross, J. W., Sebastian, I. M., and Beath, C. M., "Digital Design: It's a Journey" *MIT Sloan Center for Information Systems Research Briefing* 26, no. 4 (April 2016).

3. Danske Bank, "About Us," accessed September 6, 2012, http://www.danskebank.com/en-uk/About-us/Pages/About-us.aspx.

4. Danske Bank Group, *2019 Annual Report* (Copenhagen: Danske Bank Group, 2019), https://danskebank.com/-/media/danske-bank-com/file-cloud/2020/2/annual-report%202019.pdf?rev=ce58f68c871c451ab82c07640edbc51f&hash=091E45286122B94B1F719CEA4F23A799.

5. MobilePay, "About Us," accessed April 2, 2022, https://www.mobilepay.dk/about-us#numbers.

6. Weill, P., and Woerner, S.L., "Is Your Company Ready for a Digital Future?," *MIT Sloan Management Review* 59, no. 2 (winter 2018).

7. Danske Bank Group, *2020 Annual Report* (Copenhagen: Danske Bank Group, 2020), https://danskebank.com/-/media/danske-bank-com/file-cloud/2021/2/annual-report-2020.pdf.

8. Danske Bank, "Interim Report for the First Nine Months of 2020," November 4, 2020, https://danskebank.com/news-and-insights/news-archive/press-releases/2020/pr04112020.

9. van der Meulen, N., and Dery, K., "The Employee Experience of Digital Business Transformation," *MIT Sloan Center for Information Systems Research Briefing* 20, no. 1 (January 2020): https://cisr.mit.edu/publication/2020_0101_PathwaysEX_MeulenDery.

10. mBank has 4.7 million retail customers in Poland, plus close to 1 million customers in the Czech Republic and Slovakia, and more than 28,000 corporate customers. See mBank, "mBank in Numbers," accessed April 2, 2022, https://www.mbank.pl/en/about-us/about-mbank/.

11. International Banker, "mBank: Leading the New Wave of Innovation, Digitalization and Competitiveness in Polish Banking," March 9, 2020, https://internationalbanker.com/banking/mbank-leading-the-new-wave-of-innovation-digitalisation-and-competitiveness-in-polish-banking/.

12. Fonstad, N. O., Woerner, S. L., and Weill, P., "mBank: Creating the Digital Bank," *MIT Sloan CISR Research Briefing* 15, no. 10 (October 2015): https://cisr.mit.edu/publication/2015_1001_mBank_FonstadWoernerWeill.

13. mBank, "mBank Group in a Snapshot," accessed April 2, 2022, https://www.mbank.pl/pdf/relacje-inwestorskie/factsheet_mbankgroup_eng.pdf.

14. Andreasyan, T., "mBank Moves into Fintech Vendor Space with New Digital Banking System," June 26, 2017, https://www.fintechfutures.com

/2017/06/mbank-moves-into-fintech-vendor-space-with-new-digital-banking
-system/

15. For more information on the strategic goals, see mBank, "Growth
Fueled by Our Clients—New Strategy for 2020–2023," accessed April 2, 2022,
https://www.mbank.pl/en/annual-report/2019/outlook/rosniemy-z-klientami
-i-dzieki-nim-strategia-na-lata-2020-2023/.

16. Net-promoter score (NPS) is a single-item market metric widely used
to measure customer experience. See Reichheld, F. F., "The One Number
You Need to Grow," *Harvard Business Review*, December 2003, https://
hbr.org/2003/12/the-one-number-you-need-to-grow; NICE Satmetrix
NPS Methodology, https://www.satmetrix.com/holistic-voc-solution/nps
-methodology.

17. BBVA Group, *BBVA Group First Quarter 2021* (Birmingham, AL:
BBVA Compass, 2021), https://shareholdersandinvestors.bbva.com/wp
-content/uploads/2021/05/1Q21-BBVA-Corporate-Presentation-.pdf.

18. BBVA, "BBVA, Named Best Bank in Europe and Latin America for
Innovation in Digital Banking," August 3, 2020, https://www.bbva.com/en
/bbva-named-best-bank-in-europe-and-latin-america-for-innovation-in
-digital-banking/.

19. Fonstad, N. O., and Salonen, J., "Four Changes: How BBVA Generated Greater Strategic Value," MIT Sloan CISR Working Paper, no. 452 (October 2021): https://cisr.mit.edu/publication/MIT_CISRwp452_BBVA-SDA
_FonstadSalonen.

20. ING Group, "Transformation Update," Investor Day 2019, March 25,
2019, https://www.ing.com/Investor-relations/Presentations/Investor-Day
-presentations/2019/ING-Investor-Day-2019-Transformation-update.htm.

21. Weill and Woerner, "Is Your Company Ready for a Digital Future?"

22. Ross, J. W., Weill, P., and Robertson, D. C., *Enterprise Architecture
as Strategy: Creating a Foundation for Business Execution* (Boston: Harvard
Business School Press, 2006), 61–64.

23. ING Group, "Transformation Update."

24. ING 2017 Annual Report, https://www.ing.com/Investor-relations
/Financial-performance/Annual-reports.htm; "Scotiabank to Buy ING Bank
of Canada for $3.1B," August 29, 2012, https://www.cbc.ca/news/business
/scotiabank-to-buy-ing-bank-of-canada-for-3-1b-1.1160516; "ING Direct
to Become 'Capital One 360,' but Promises to Remain the Same," November
7, 2012, https://www.americanbanker.com/news/ing-direct-to-become-capital
-one-360; and "ING to Sell ING Direct UK to Barclays," press release,
October 9, 2012, https://www.ing.com/Newsroom/News/Press-releases
/PROld/ING-to-sell-ING-Direct-UK-to-Barclays.htm.

25. We suggest executive roles to lead transformations on each pathway based on correlations with the most complete transformations in the 2017 survey.

26. Woerner, S. L., Weill, P., and Diaz Baquero, A. P., "Coordinating Multiple Pathways for Transformation Progress," *MIT Sloan CISR Research Briefing* 22, no. 4 (April 2022): https://cisr.mit.edu/publication/2022_0401 _MultiplePathways_WoernerWeillDiazBaquero.

27. Provided by company, compiled based on reports available at "Financial results," Investor Relations, Grupo Bancolombia, https://www .grupobancolombia.com/investor-relations/financial-information/quarter -results.

28. The source for 10 million users was executive interviews.

29. Number of non-bank correspondents from unpublished company documents; used with permission. Bancolombia ATM details from Bancolombia S.A., "Corporate Presentation," January 2022, p. 2, https://www .grupobancolombia.com/wcm/connect/www.grupobancolombia.com15880 /4da24cd8-e940-46fa-a83f-e3e2e5be6788/Corporate+Presentation.pdf?MOD =AJPERES&CVID=nZHOCJm.

30. MIT CISR 2019 TMT and Transformation Survey (N = 1,311). We compared firms on multiple pathways that were well-coordinated versus firms on multiple pathways that were not coordinated on several measures using a difference of means test. The items described were the three measures that had the largest differences. The differences were significant at the p < .05 level.

31. See, for instance, Sambamurthy, V., and Zmud, R. W., "Arrangements for Information Technology Governance: A Theory of Multiple Contingencies," *MIS Quarterly* 23, no. 2 (June 1999): 261–290; and Weill, P., and Ross, J. W., *IT Governance: How Top Performers Manage IT Decision Rights for Superior Results* (Boston: Harvard Business School Press, 2004).

32. A digital platform "standardizes and automates [core business] processes, thereby increasing reliability, decreasing operational costs, and ensuring quality," as per Weill, P., and Ross, J. W., *IT Savvy: What Top Executives Must Know to Go from Pain to Gain* (Boston: Harvard Business Press, 2009), 16.

33. Girod, S. J. G., and Karim, S. "Restructure or Reconfigure?," *Harvard Business Review*, March–April 2017.

34. Weill, P., and Woerner, S. L., *What's Your Digital Business Model? Six Questions to Help You Build the Next-Generation Enterprise* (Boston: Harvard Business Review Press, May 2018).

Notes

35. Ensor, B., "BBVA Tops Forrester's 2019 Global Mobile Banking App Reviews," Forrester, September 24, 2019, https://go.forrester.com/blogs/bbva-tops-forresters-2019-global-mobile-banking-app-reviews/.

36. BBVA, "BBVA Earns €1.32 Billion in 4Q20, its Best Quarterly Result in Two Years," January 29, 2021, https://www.bbva.com/en/results-4q20/.

37. Wixom, B.H., and Someh, I., "Accelerating Data-Driven Transformation at BBVA," *MIT Sloan CISR Research Briefing* 13, no. 7 (July 2018): https://cisr.mit.edu/publication/2018_0701_DataDrivenBBVA_WixomSomeh.

38. BBVA, "BBVA's Journey to Become a Digital, Data-Driven Bank," June 11, 2021, https://www.bbva.com/en/bbvas-journey-to-become-a-digital-data-driven-bank/.

Chapter 3

1. MIT CISR 2019 TMT and Transformation Survey (N = 1,311).

2. Digital threat was assessed in the MIT CISR 2017 Digital Pathways Survey (N = 400).

3. MIT CISR 2019 TMT and Transformation Survey (N = 1,311).

4. Weill, P., and Ross, J. W., *IT Savvy: What Top Executives Must Know to Go from Pain to Gain* (Boston: Harvard Business Press, 2009); Parker, G. G., van Alstyne, M., and Choudary, S. P., *Platform Revolution: How Networked Markets Are Transforming the Economy* (New York: W. W. Norton, 2017); Ross, J. W., Beath, C. M., and Nelson, R., "The Digital Operating Model: Building a Componentized Organization," *MIT Sloan CISR Research Briefing* 20, no. 6 (June 18, 2020): https://cisr.mit.edu/publication/2020_0601_BuildingComponentizedOrganization_RossBeathNelson.

5. Someh, I. A., Wixom, B. H., and Gregory, R. W., "The Australian Taxation Office: Creating Value with Advanced Analytics," MIT Sloan CISR Working Paper, no. 447 (November 2020): https://cisr.mit.edu/publication/MIT_CISRwp447_ATOAdvancedAnalytics_SomehWixomGregory.

6. Kaiser Permanente, "Fast Facts," December 31, 2021, https://about.kaiserpermanente.org/who-we-are/fast-facts.

7. Kagan, M., Sebastian, I. M., and Ross, J. W., "Kaiser Permanente: Executing a Consumer Digital Strategy," MIT Sloan CISR Working Paper, no. 405 (2016): https://cisr.mit.edu/publication/MIT_CISRwp408_KaiserPermanente_KaganSebastianRoss.

8. Prat Vemana, email message to the authors as part of case study approval, April 29, 2022.

9. Diane Comer, email message to the authors as part of case study approval, April 29, 2022.

10. Funahashi, T., Borgo L., and Joshi, N., "Saving Lives with Virtual Cardiac Rehabilitation," *NEJM Catalyst Innovations in Care Delivery*, August 28, 2019, https://catalyst.nejm.org/doi/full/10.1056/CAT.19.0624, https://catalyst .nejm.org/doi/full/10.1056/CAT.19.0624; Kaiser Permanente, "Reducing Secondary Cardiac Events with Virtual Cardiac Rehab," August 28, 2019, https://about.kaiserpermanente.org/our-story/news/announcements/-reducing -secondary-cardiac-events-with-virtual-cardiac-rehab.

11. Sebastian, I. M., Weill, P., and Woerner, S. L., "Three Types of Value Drive Performance in Digital Business," MIT Sloan CISR Research Briefing no. XXI-3 (March 18, 2021): https://cisr.mit.edu/publication/2021_0301 _ValueinDigitalBusiness_SebastianWeillWoerner.

12. Funahashi, Borgo, and Joshi, "Saving Lives with Virtual Cardiac Rehabilitation."

13. Kagan, Sebastian, and Ross, "Kaiser Permanente."

14. Sebastian, Weill, and Woerner, "Three Types of Value Drive Performance in Digital Business."

15. Prat Vemana, interview with Ina Sebastian (author), March 11, 2020.

16. Tetra Pak, "Tetra Pak in Figures," January 1, 2021, https://www.tetrapak .com/about-tetra-pak/the-company/facts-figures; van der Meulen, M., Weill, P., and Woerner, S. L., "Managing Organizational Explosions during Digital Business Transformations," *MIS Quarterly Executive*, September 2020; Weill, P., Woerner, S. L., and van der Meulen, N., "Four Pathways to 'Future Ready' that Pay Off," *European Business Review*, March–April 2019.

17. Tetra Pak, "Tetra Pak Introduces the 'Factory of the Future' with Human and AI Collaboration at Its Core," March 29, 2019, https://www .tetrapak.com/en-us/about-tetra-pak/news-and-events/newsarchive/factory -of-the-future.

18. Tetra Pak, "Tetra Pak Launches Connected Packaging Platform," April 3, 2019, https://www.tetrapak.com/en-us/about-tetra-pak/news-and -events/newsarchive/connected-packaging-platform.

19. Tetra Pak, "Tetra Pak Calls for Collaborative Innovation to Tackle Sustainability Challenges in the Food Packaging Industry," January 25, 2021, https://www.tetrapak.com/en-us/about-tetra-pak/news-and-events /newsarchive/collaborative-innovation-tackle-sustainability-challenges-food -packaging-industry.

20. Sebastian, I. M., Weill, P., and Woerner, S. L., "Driving Growth in Digital Ecosystems," *MIT Sloan Management Review*, August 18, 2020,

https://sloanreview.mit.edu/article/driving-growth-in-digital-ecosystems/;
Tetra Pak, "Voices of Innovation: The Power of Partnership," January 25,
2021, https://www.youtube.com/playlist?list=PLR9c4Ljeb6khqftcD7HrOxw
UhiWZQ53xx.

Chapter 4

1. MIT CISR 2019 TMT and Transformation Survey (N = 1,311).

2. MIT CISR 2019 TMT and Transformation Survey (N = 1,311).

3. Dery, K., and van der Meulen, N., "The Employee Experience of Digital Business Transformation," *MIT Sloan CISR Research Briefing* 20, no. 1 (January 2020): https://cisr.mit.edu/publication/2020_0101_PathwaysEX _MeulenDery.

4. The CarMax description is drawn primarily on the MIT Sloan CISR case study by Ross, J. W., Beath, C. M., and Nelson, R., "Redesigning CarMax to Deliver an Omni-Channel Customer Experience," MIT Sloan CISR Working Paper, no. 442 (June 18, 2020): https://cisr.mit.edu/publication /MIT_CISRwp442_CarMax_RossBeathNelson; and CarMax, "Analyst Day 2021," May 6, 2021, https://investors.carmax.com/news-and-events/events -and-presentations/carmax-analyst-day/default.aspx; https://s27.q4cdn.com /743947716/files/doc_presentations/2021/05/07/CarMax-Analyst-Day-2021 -Summary.pdf.

5. CarMax, "Our Purpose," accessed April 4, 2022, www.carmax.com /about-carmax.

6. CarMax, *CarMax Annual Report 2021* (Richmond, VA: Carmax, 2021), https://s27.q4cdn.com/743947716/files/doc_financials/2021/ar/KMX -FY21-Annual-Report.pdf.

7. CarMax has received awards such as *Fortune* magazine's 100 Best Companies to Work For for seventeen consecutive years as well as *Forbes'* Best Workplaces for Diversity: CarMax, *Carmax Annual Report 2021*, https://s27.q4cdn.com/743947716/files/doc_financials/2021/ar/KMX-FY21 -Annual-Report.pdf; Carmax, "Company Recognition," accessed April 4, 2022, http://media.carmax.com/Recognition/.

8. Shamim Mohammad, email to the authors, April 12, 2022.

9. Ross, Beath, and Nelson, "Redesigning CarMax."

10. Ross, Beath, and Nelson, "Redesigning CarMax."

11. Ross, Beath, and Nelson, "Redesigning CarMax."

12. Ross, Beath, and Nelson, "Redesigning CarMax."

13. CarMax, "CarMax Analyst Day 2021."

14. The CEMEX case study draws on many sources and is used with permission including van der Meulen, N., Weill, P., and Woerner, S. L., "Managing Organizational Explosions during Digital Business Transformations," *MIS Quarterly Executive*, September 2020, 165–182; Weill, P., Woerner, S. L., and van der Meulen, N., "Four Pathways to 'Future Ready' that Pay Off," *European Business Review*, March–April 2019, 11–15; interactions with the CEMEX top management team in MIT Sloan Executive Education sessions; MIT CISR Surveys and interviews; CEMEX.com; and CEMEX Annual Reports and Quarterly Results.

15. van der Meulen, Weill, and Woerner, "Managing Organizational Explosions."

16. CEMEX Annual Report 2019, https://www.cemex.com/documents /20143/49694544/IntegratedReport2019.pdf/4e1b2519-b75f-e61a-7cce -2a2f2f6f09dc; CEMEX Second Quarter 2020 Results, https://www.cemex .com/documents/20143/49897099/2Q20results_English.pdf/42519285-1974 -b582-c96c-8e6e455831d7.

17. CEMEX Third Quarter 2020 Results, https://www.cemex.com /documents/20143/49897099/3Q20results_English.pdf/b53e9747-672f-59fb -f8e8-a26342e32132.

18. The disruptive success of the CEMEX Go platform in the building materials industry, which has been recognized by LOGISTIK HEUTE through the Supply Chain Management Award 2018, has led CEMEX to further monetize the platform by licensing it to other global industry participants. For more information on the LOGISTIK HEUTE award, see "CEMEX Go Wins Renowned German Award," CEMEX press release, December 6, 2018, https://www.cemex.com/press-releases-2018/-/asset_publisher /aKEb3AUF78Y0/content/cemex-go-wins-renowned-german-award.

19. "CEMEX Launches Construrama Online Store," CEMEX press release, June 6, 2018, https://apnews.com/press-release/business-wire/business -lifestyle-mexico-materials-industry-562f012429874ae49a54de9b90bb80d2.

20. CEMEX Go Developer Center and use cases, https://developers .cemexgo.com, https://developers.cemexgo.com/usecases0; CEMEX 2019 Annual Report, https://www.cemex.com/documents/20143/49694544 /IntegratedReport2019.pdf/4e1b2519-b75f-e61a-7cce-2a2f2f6f09dc.

21. "CEMEX Presents CEMEX Go Developer Center," CEMEX press release, April 4, 2019, https://www.cemex.com/press-releases-2019/-/asset _publisher/sixj9tAnl3LW/content/cemex-presents-cemex-go-developer -center?_com_liferay_asset_publisher_web_portlet_AssetPublisherPortlet _INSTANCE_sixj9tAnl3LW_redirect=https%3A%2F%2Fwww.cemex

.com%3A443%2Fpress-releases-2019%3Fp_p_id%3Dcom_liferay
_asset_publisher_web_portlet_AssetPublisherPortlet_INSTANCE
_sixj9tAnl3LW%26p_p_lifecycle%3D0%26p_p_state%3Dnormal%26p
_p_mode%3Dview%26_com_liferay_asset_publisher_web_portlet
_AssetPublisherPortlet_INSTANCE_sixj9tAnl3LW_cur%3D0%26p
_r_p_resetCur%3Dfalse%26_com_liferay_asset_publisher_web
_portlet_AssetPublisherPortlet_INSTANCE_sixj9tAnl3LW_asset
EntryId%3D47830218.

22. "CEMEX Ventures Invests in Carbon Capture Tech of the Future,"
CEMEX press release, August 3, 2021, https://www.cemexventures.com
/carbon-capture-technology/.

23. "CEMEX Joins OpenBuilt to Accelerate Digital Transformation of the
Construction Industry," CEMEX press release, April 14, 2021, https://www
.cemex.com/-/cemex-joins-openbuilt-to-accelerate-digital-transformation-of
-the-construction-industry.

24. van der Meulen, Weill, and Woerner, "Managing Organizational
Explosions."

25. Responses from EVP administration and organization Luis Hernandez
Echavez and CEO Fernando González to email questions from us on July 6,
2021.

26. Fernando González, email message to author, January 30, 2021.

Chapter 5

1. MIT CISR 2019 TMT and Transformation Survey (N = 1,311). Survey
respondents identified the industry of their firms. Industries were consolidated to reflect North American Industry Classification System (NAICS)
categories. Consumer equals hospitality, travel, restaurants, retail, arts, entertainment, and recreation.

2. "World's Best Digital Bank 2018: DBS," Euromoney, July 11, 2018,
https://www.euromoney.com/article/b18k8wtzv7v23d/world39s-best-digital
-bank-2018-dbs.

3. "DBS Named Best Bank in the World," DBS, August 24, 2018, https://
www.dbs.com/newsroom/DBS_named_Best_Bank_in_the_World.

4. Working with Siew Kien Sia and his colleagues at the Nanyang Business School in Singapore, Peter Weill published two case studies and two
articles based on many interviews with DBS executives and reviewing many
internal DBS documents. We gratefully acknowledge the partnership with
DBS to complete and publish this analysis. See Sia, S. K., Weill, P., and

Zhang, N., "Designing a Future-Ready Enterprise: The Digital Transformation of DBS Bank," *California Management Review* (March 2021) (this section of the book draws heavily on this article); Sia, S. K., Soh, C., Weill, P.,
and Chong, Y., "Rewiring the Enterprise for Digital Innovation: The Case of
DBS Bank," Nanyang Technological University, Nanyang Business School,
and the Asian Business Case Centre, pub no. ABCC-2015-004, June 2015;
Sia, S. K., Weill, P., and Xu, M., "DBS: From the 'World's Best Bank' to
Building the Future-Ready Enterprise," MIT Sloan CISR Working Paper,
no. 436 (March 18, 2019), https://cisr.mit.edu/publication/MIT_CISRwp436
_DBS-FutureReadyEnterprise_SiaWeillXu; and Weill, P., Sia, S. K., and
Soh, C., "How DBS Pursued a Digital Business Strategy," *MIS Quarterly
Executive* 15, no. 2 (2016): 105–121.

　　5. See DBS, "Fixed Income Investor Presentation," accessed April 5,
2022, https://www.dbs.com/iwov-resources/images/investors/overview
/Fixed%20income%20investor%20presentation%201H21_vF.pdf?productId
=jx3sjprr. 2014 average currency exchange rate is from exchangerates
.org.uk (https://www.exchangerates.org.uk/SGD-USD-spot-exchange-
rates-history-2014.html#:~:text=Average%20exchange%20rate%20in%20
2014%3A%200.7893%20USD). The 2021 average currency exchange rate is
from exchangerates.org.uk (https://www.exchangerates.org.uk/SGD-USD
-spot-exchange-rates-history-2021.html#:~:text=Average%20exchange%20
rate%20in%202021%3A%200.7442%20USD).

　　6. Sia, Weill, and Zhang, "Designing a Future-Ready Enterprise."

　　7. Sia, Weill, and Zhang, "Designing a Future-Ready Enterprise."

　　8. Sia, Weill, and Zhang, "Designing a Future-Ready Enterprise."

　　9. Sia, Weill, and Xu, "DBS: From the 'World's Best Bank.'"

　　10. DBS, *Annual Report 2017* (Singapore: DBS, 2017), https://www.dbs
.com/annualreports/2017/index.html.

　　11. Sia, Weill, and Xu, "DBS: From the 'World's Best Bank.'"

　　12. Sia, Weill, and Xu, "DBS: From the 'World's Best Bank.'"

　　13. DBS, "Reimagining Banking, DBS Launches World's Largest Banking API Developer Platform," November 2, 2017, https://www.dbs.com
/newsroom/Reimagining_banking_DBS_launches_worlds_largest_banking
_API_developer_platform.

　　14. Sia, Weill, and Zhang, "Designing a Future-Ready Enterprise."

　　15. Sia, Weill, and Zhang, "Designing a Future-Ready Enterprise."

　　16. Sia, Weill, and Xu, "DBS: From the 'World's Best Bank.'"

　　17. Cobban, P., "DBS' Digital Transformation Journey to Become the
World's Best Bank," Cuscal Curious Thinkers Virtual Program, June 22,

2021. The thirty-three platforms figure is also noted in Tan, A., "DBS Bank Goes Big on Open Source," ComputerWeekly.com, June 25, 2019, https://www.computerweekly.com/news/252465653/DBS-Bank-goes-big-on-open-source

18. A two-in-a-box system or approach refers to a management approach in which two (or more) people are given equal leadership authority and responsibility for a task or set of tasks, often in complementary roles.

19. Sia, Weill, and Xu, "DBS: From the 'World's Best Bank.'"

20. Sia, Weill, and Xu, "DBS: From the 'World's Best Bank.'"

21. DBS, "Banking without Branches, DBS digibank India Gains 1m Customers in a Year," June 8, 2017, https://www.dbs.com/innovation/dbs-innovates/banking-without-branches-dbs-digibank-india-gains-1m-customers-in-a-year.html.

22. DBS, "Banking without Branches."

23. Sia, Weill, and Xu, "DBS: From the 'World's Best Bank.'"

24. MIT CISR studied KPN over several years, led by our colleague Dr. Nick van der Meulen. This section draws heavily on three publications: van der Meulen, N., Weill, P., and Woerner, S. L., "Managing Organizational Explosions during Digital Business Transformations," *MIS Quarterly Executive*, September 2020, 165–182; Weill, P., Woerner, S. L., and van der Meulen, N., "Four Pathways to 'Future Ready' that Pay Off," *European Business Review* (March–April 2019): 11–15; van de Meulen, N., Weill, P., and Woerner, S. L., "Digital Transformation at KPMG: Navigating Organizational Disruption," MIT Sloan CISR Case Study Working Paper, no. 431 (August 2018), https://cisr.mit.edu/publication/MIT_CISRwp431_PathwaysKPN_VanderMeulenWeillWoerner.

25. "KPN Integrated Annual Report 2020: Accelerating Digitalization of the Netherlands" (Amsterdam: KPN, 2020), p. 9, https://ir.kpn.com/download/companies/koninkpnnv/Results/KPN_IR_2020_Single_navigation.pdf.

26. "KPN Integrated Annual Report 2020: Accelerating Digitalization of the Netherlands."

27. An over-the-top media service is a streaming service offered directly to consumers via the internet. Over-the-top firms bypass cable, broadcast, and satellite television platforms—the firms that traditionally act as a controller or distributor of such content. While commonly applied to video-on-demand platforms, the term also refers to audio streaming, messaging services, and internet-based voice calling solutions.

28. On average, European telecom firms' revenues declined by 33 percent between 2008 and 2017. For an overview of these economic developments, see GSMA Europe, "The Mobile Economy—Europe 2017,"

October 17, 2017, https://www.gsma.com/gsmaeurope/resources/mobile -economy-europe-2017/; and GSMA, "Mobile Economy Europe 2013," September 5, 2013, https://www.gsmaintelligence.com/research/?file=6b321d25 537f3bf708ffa34fabcdbf91&download.

29. van der Meulen, Weill, and Woerner, "Managing Organizational Explosions."

30. van der Meulen, Weill, and Woerner, "Digital Transformation at KPMG."

31. "KPN Integrated Annual Report 2020: Accelerating Digitalization of the Netherlands," p. 7, https://ir.kpn.com/download/companies/koninkpnnv /Results/KPN_IR_2020_Single_navigation.pdf.

Chapter 6

1. Climate FieldView, "Climate FieldView," accessed April 7, 2022, https://climate.com/https://dev.fieldview.com.

2. FieldView for Developers, "More Visibility for Your Solutions," accessed April 7, 2022, https://dev.fieldview.com.

3. Bayer Global, "Advancing Sustainability and Efficiency: Are You Prepared for the Future of Agriculture?" June 21, 2021, https://www.bayer.com /en/investors/agriculture-megatrends.

4. Climate FieldView, "Bayer, Microsoft Enter into Strategic Partnership to Optimize and Advance Digital Capabilities for Food, Feed, Fuel, Fiber Value Chain," press release, November 17, 2021, https://climate.com/press -releases/bayer-microsoft-strategic-partnership/.

5. Eickhoff, T., and Williams, J., "The Beginning of What's Next: The 2022 Digital Farming Research Pipeline," Climate FieldView, February 15, 2022, https://climate.com/tech-at-climate-corp/the-beginning-of-what-s-next -the-2022-digital-farming-research-pipeline/.

6. Ping An Healthcare and Technology Company Limited, "'Easier, Faster, and More Affordable': Ping An Good Doctor's New Strategy Builds on Solid Foundation," Cision PR Newswire, October 24, 2021, https://www .prnewswire.com/news-releases/easier-faster-and-more-affordable-ping-an -good-doctors-new-strategy-builds-on-solid-foundation-301407238.html.

7. Currency conversion using Google, pulled on March 1, 2022.

8. Ping An Healthcare and Technology Company Limited, "Ping An Good Doctor Posts 39% Revenue Growth in the First Half of 2021; Revenue from Medical Services Grows 50.6%; Total Number of Registered Users Reaches 400 Million," Cision PR Newswire, August 24, 2021, https:// www.prnewswire.com/news-releases/ping-an-good-doctor-posts-39 -revenue-growth-in-the-first-half-of-2021-revenue-from-medical-services

-grows-50-6-total-number-of-registered-users-reaches-400-million
-301361754.html.

9. Ping An Healthcare and Technology Company Limited, "'Easier,
Faster and More Affordable.'"

10. Email from Ana Maria Bonomi Barufi, Innovation Research Manager, Banco Bradesco, on behalf of the next team, to Ina Sebastian (author),
April 30, 2022.

11. The Bancolombia and Nequi details can be found in Diaz Baquero,
A. P., and Woerner, S. L., "Bancolombia: Coordinating Multiple Digital
Transformations," MIT Sloan CISR Working Paper, no. 455 (April 2022),
https://cisr.mit.edu/publication/MIT_CISRwp455_Bancolombia
_DiazBaqueroWoerner.

12. Weill, P., and Woerner, S. L., *What's Your Digital Business Model? Six
Questions to Help You Build the Next-Generation Enterprise* (Boston: Harvard Business Review Press, 2018).

13. Schneider Electric, "Schneider Electric Half Year 2021 Results—
July 30, 2021," July 30, 2021, https://www.se.com/ww/en/assets/564
/document/220698/presentation-half-year-results-2021.pdf.

14. Weill, P., Woerner, S. L., and Diaz Baquero, A. P., "Hello Domains,
Goodbye Industries," *MIT Sloan Center for Information Systems Research
Briefing* 21, no. 1 (January 2021), https://cisr.mit.edu/publication/2021_0101
_HelloDomains_WeillWoernerDiaz.

15. Schneider Electric SE, "Universal Registration Document 2019,"
March 17, 2020, https://www.se.com/ww/en/assets/564/document/124836
/annual-report-2019-en.pdf.

16. Tricoire, J.-P., "Capital Markets Day," Schneider Electric, June 26,
2019, https://www.se.com/ww/en/assets/564/document/46841/26
-presentation-strategy-investor-day-2019.pdf.

17. Fidelity, "Navigating the College Journey," accessed April 7, 2022,
https://myguidance.fidelity.com/ftgw/pna/public/lifeevents/content/sending
-child-to-college/overview; Fidelity, "Attending College," accessed April 7,
2022, https://myguidance.fidelity.com/ftgw/pna/public/lifeevents/content
/sending-child-to-college/overview/attending-college.

18. Researcher interpretation based on information from Shopify, "Shopify Q2 2020 Results" (Shopify Q2 2020 Financial Results
Conference Call, July 29, 2020), https://s27.q4cdn.com/572064924
/files/doc_downloads/2020/Shopify-Investor-Deck-Q2-2020.pdf, and
from the Shopify website, https://www.shopify.com/. Financial information from Shopify, "Q4 2021 Results," February 2022, https://s27.q4cdn

.com/572064924/files/doc_financials/2021/q4/Shopify-Investor-Deck-Q4
-2021.pdf.

19. Tricoire, "Capital Markets Day," 11 and 17.

20. Maersk, *2021 Annual Report* (Copenhagen: A. P. Moller-Maersk,
2021), https://investor.maersk.com/static-files/b4df47ef-3977-412b-8e3c
-bc2f02bb4a5f. All figures as of December 31, 2021.

21. TradeLens, "Where We Are Today," accessed April 7, 2022, https://tour
.tradelens.com/status; Maersk, *2019 Annual Report* (Copenhagen:
A. P. Moller-Maersk, 2019), https://investor.maersk.com/static-files/984a2b93
-0035-40d3-9cae-77161c9a36e0.

22. This case vignette is based on fourteen interviews with executives between 2019 and 2022, and on public sources. This case draws
heavily on Sebastian, I. M., Weill, P., and Woerner, S. L., "Three Types
of Value Driver Performance in Digital Business," MIT Sloan CISR Research Briefing no. XXI-3, https://cisr.mit.edu/publication/2021_0301
_ValueinDigitalBusiness_SebastianWeillWoerner.

23. Maersk, *2020 Annual Report* (Copenhagen: A. P. Moller-Maersk,
2020), https://investor.maersk.com/static-files/97a03c29-46a2-4e84-9b7e
-12d4ee451361; TradeLens, "Network," https://www.tradelens.com/ecosystem.

24. Email from Daniel Wilson, head of strategy and operations, TradeLens,
GTD Solution, to one of the authors, March 24, 2022.

25. Pico, S., "Søren Skou Expects Growth from Maersk's Blockchain Venture in 2021," *ShippingWatch*, December 1, 2020, https://shippingwatch.com
/carriers/Container/article12596226.ece.

26. Maersk, *2019 Annual Report* (Copenhagen: A. P. Moller-Maersk,
2019), https://investor.maersk.com/static-files/984a2b93-0035-40d3-9cae
-77161c9a36e0.

27. TradeLens, "CMA CGM and MSC Complete TradeLens Integration
and Join as Foundation Carriers," press release, October 15, 2020, https://
www.tradelens.com/press-releases/cma-cgm-and-msc-complete-tradelens
-integration-and-join-as-foundation-carriers.

28. This case draws heavily on van der Meulen, N., Weill, P., and
Woerner, S. L., "Managing Organizational Explosions during Digital
Business Transformations," *MIS Quarterly Executive*, September 2020,
165–182.

29. Domain Group, "About Domain Group," accessed April 8, 2022,
https://www.domain.com.au/group/.

30. van der Meulen, Weill, and Woerner, "Managing Organizational Explosions during Digital Business Transformations," 165–182.

Notes

31. For more on digital partnering, see Sebastian, I. M., Weill, P., and Woerner, S. L., "Partnering to Grow in the Digital Era," *European Business Review*, March–April 2020, 61–65.

Chapter 7

1. For a definition of *digital savvy* and the relationship to firm performance, see Weill, P., Woerner, S. L., and Shah, A.M., "Does Your C-Suite Have Enough Digital Smarts?" *MIT Sloan Management Review*, Spring 2021, 63–67.

2. Weill, Woerner, and Shah, "Does Your C-Suite Have Enough Digital Smarts?"

3. Weill, Woerner, and Shah, "Does Your C-Suite Have Enough Digital Smarts?"

4. The financial impacts of having a digitally savvy board referenced throughout this section draw from MIT CISR research described in Weill, P., Apel, T., Woerner, S. L., and Banner, J. S., "Assessing the Impact of a Digitally Savvy Board on Firm Performance," MIT Sloan CISR Working Paper, no. 433 (January 2019): https://cisr.mit.edu/publication/MIT_CISRwp433_DigitallySavvyBoards_WeillApelWoernerBanner; and Weill, P., Apel, T., Woerner, S. L., and Banner, J. S., "It Pays to Have a Digitally Savvy Board," *MIT Sloan Management Review*, March 12, 2019. We studied the boards of all US-listed firms with more than $1 billion in revenues that had six or more directors.

5. Principal Financial Group, "Profile and Offerings," accessed April 8, 2022, https://www.principal.com/about-us/our-company/profile-and-offerings.

6. Standard Bank Group, "Our Values and Code of Ethics," accessed April 8, 2022, https://www.standardbank.com/sbg/standard-bank-group/who-we-are/our-values-and-code-of-ethics.

7. Cochlear, "About Us," accessed April 8, 2022, https://www.cochlear.com/au/en/about-us.

8. Schneider Electric, "Company Profile," accessed April 8, 2022, https://www.se.com/us/en/about-us/company-profile/.

9. Scott, M., "Top Company Profile: Schneider Electric Leads Decarbonizing Megatrend," *Corporate Knights*, January 25, 2021, https://www.corporateknights.com/leadership/top-company-profile-schneider-electric-leads-decarbonizing-megatrend25289/.

10. Tetra Pak, "Our Identity and Values," accessed April 8, 2022, https://www.tetrapak.com/about-tetra-pak/the-company/our-identity-and-values.

11. DBS, "Our Vision," accessed April 8, 2022, https://www.dbs.com /about-us/who-we-are/our-vision.

12. TradeLens, "Digitizing the Global Supply Chain," accessed April 8, 2022, https://www.tradelens.com/about.

13. Principal Financial Group, "About Us," accessed May 1, 2022, https:// www.principal.com/about-us.

14. CarMax, "Our Purpose," accessed April 8, 2022, www.carmax.com /about-carmax.

15. We identified the ten future-ready capabilities through a series of interviews and conversations, conducted between 2015 and 2019, on digital transformation with senior executives globally. We quantified the relationships between capabilities and value using data from the MIT CISR 2019 Top Management Teams and Transformation Survey (N = 1,311) and followed up with further interviews between 2019 and 2022.

16. Weill, P., and Woerner, S.L., *What's Your Digital Business Model? Six Questions to Help You Build the Next-Generation Enterprise* (Boston: Harvard Business Review Press, 2018).

17. Sebastian, I. M., Weill, P., Woerner, S. L., "Driving Growth in Digital Ecosystems," *MIT Sloan Management Review*, Fall 2020, Reprint 62127, https://sloanreview.mit.edu/article/driving-growth-in-digital -ecosystems/.

18. Wixom, B. H., and Ross, J. W., "How to Monetize Your Data," *MIT Sloan Management Review*, Spring 2017, Reprint 58310, https://sloanreview .mit.edu/article/how-to-monetize-your-data/.

19. Dery, K., Woerner, S. L., and Beath, C. M., "Equipping and Empowering the Future-Ready Workforce," *MIT Sloan Center for Information Systems Research Briefing* 20, no. 12 (December 2020), https://cisr.mit.edu/publication /2020_1201_FutureReadyWorkforce_DeryWoernerBeath.

20. Wixom, B. H., and Someh, I. A., "Accelerating Data-Driven Transformation at BBVA," *MIT Sloan Center for Information Systems Research Briefing* 18, no. 7 (July 2018), https://cisr.mit.edu/publication/2018_0701 _DataDrivenBBVA_WixomSomeh.

21. See figure 5 in Sia, S. K., Weill, P., and Xu, M., "DBS: From the 'World's Best Bank' to Building the Future-Ready Enterprise," Nanyang Business School, December 2018, Ref No.: ABCC-2019-001, https://cisr.mit.edu /publication/MIT_CISRwp436_DBS-FutureReadyEnterprise_SiaWeillXu.

22. Fonstad, N. O., "Innovating Greater Value Faster by Taking Time to Learn," *MIT Sloan Center for Information Systems Research Briefing* 20, no. 2, February 2020, https://cisr.mit.edu/publication/2020_0201 _InnovatingGreaterValueFaster_Fonstad.

23. Sebastian, I. M., Weill, P., and Woerner, S. L., "Three Types of Value Drive Performance in Digital Business," *MIT Sloan Center for Information Systems Research Briefing* 21, no. 3 (March 2021), https://cisr.mit.edu /publication/2021_0301_ValueinDigitalBusiness_SebastianWeillWoerner.

24. This case draws heavily on Weill, P., and Woerner, S. L., "Dashboarding Pays Off," *MIT Sloan Center for Information Systems Research Briefing*, no. XXII-1, January 20, 2022: https://cisr.mit.edu/publication/2022_0101 _Dashboarding_WeillWoerner. Revenues are from Schneider Electric SE, "Enabling a Sustainable Future, 2021 Universal Registration Document," https://www.se.com/ww/en/assets/564/document/319364/2021-universal -registration-document.pdf.

25. Tricoire, J.-P., "Accelerating" (presentation, Capital Markets Day 2021, Rueil-Malmaison, France, November 30, 2021), https://www.se.com/ww/en /assets/564/document/260776/accelerating-jean-pascal-tricoire-2021-cmd.pdf.

26. Weill and Woerner, "Dashboarding Pays Off."

27. For simplicity, we have used the average scores for all pathways in the dashboard. In the actual data, there were some differences in the scores by pathway, particularly in the first third of the transformation journey (we asked respondents how far along they were on their transformation journey compared to what was presented to the board). Specifically, operations value was more important on pathway 1 and customer value was more important on pathway 2. In the second and final thirds of the transformation journey there were very few significant differences.

28. For the purposes of this exercise, assume that each of the multiple items within any score is equally important. In the actual data this is not true, but the errors from this assumption will be small.

Index

Note: Page numbers followed by *f* refer to figures, and page numbers with *n* indicate notes.

Index

Index

Index

Acknowledgments

Writing a book can be a solitary process, but we were fortunate to have the opposite experience—we have been surrounded by wonderful people. We were driven by our desire to understand how companies can succeed in the digital era. What enabled us was being part of MIT's Center for Information Systems Research (CISR). MIT CISR, which will celebrate its fiftieth anniversary in 2024, is a research center in the Sloan School of Management. We study how larger companies are going to thrive in the next era of technological change. We have a wonderful, global community of around eighty-five member companies (see cisr.mit.edu). It is the combination of MIT's strong research culture and the willingness, generosity, and openness of the companies we work with that makes the research described in this book possible. In addition to engaging with MIT CISR sponsors and patrons, we surveyed more than two thousand companies and interviewed over one hundred executives, all of whom shared their insights with us. We thank everybody involved for their critical contributions.

We are fortunate and proud to work in a rich and exciting research environment such as MIT. We have benefited from the leadership, support, and encouragement of MIT Sloan School deans David Schmittlein and Michael Cusumano, along with our IT group professorial colleagues Wanda Orlikowski, Stuart

Madnick, Thomas Malone, and Sinan Aral. It's a pleasure to work with all of you.

We were pleased to work again with Jeff Kehoe and the entire team at Harvard Business Review Press (this is our seventh book together). Jeff's suggestions strengthened the book and helped make it more compelling. A big thank you to the six anonymous reviewers—their comments highlighted areas of the book that needed work. We worked with a great graphics team, Boudewijn van Diepen from Studio van Diepen and Vincent Meertens from TIN. They asked good questions, made us think about what we really wanted to convey, and then delivered graphics that make the text sing. And we are excited to be working with Veronica Kido from Kido Communications on publicizing this book.

Every member of MIT CISR is a great colleague. The MIT CISR research team—Wanda Orlikowski, Barb Wixom, Nils Fonstad, Nick van der Meulen, Cynthia Beath, and, most recently, Kristine Dery, Jeanne Ross, and Aman Shah—encourage us, debate with us, and help us clarify insights. The MIT CISR administrative team is among the best in the business. Chris Foglia, Dorothea Gray, Cheryl Miller, and (until lately) Leslie Owens and Amber Franey communicate with sponsors and patrons, plan events, support research projects, get research findings out the door, and generally take care of everything needed. We could not do our research or have a research center without their partnership. We cannot thank you all enough! Cheryl Miller also took on the job of helping us find and manage a graphics team. Getting the graphics into shape was a creative, detail-oriented job, and we appreciate Cheryl's effort—it shows.

We gratefully acknowledge the support of the companies that are currently MIT CISR's sponsors and patrons. These large companies are the core of the MIT CISR community, and their support goes beyond funding our research to offering access, providing data, and agreeing to be case study examples. We are honored to have the opportunity to work with their leaders. They have a passion for the opportunities and challenges that digital technologies create along with a willingness to share their experiences, which helps us develop insights and understand best practices. We bounce ideas off them and work with them to identify the big issues facing their companies. Most important, we conduct workshops, at their offices and online, to really dig into how they tackle those issues, combining our research with their experience. It is a privilege to work with them, and it is essential to our research process. It is the iteration of presentations, workshops, discussions, debates, and the occasional argument that helps us refine insights and hit key messages. The past two years have been especially challenging for our member companies. Each one of them had to pivot to deal with Covid-19, usually accelerating transformation plans by months, if not years; and time and attention were in short supply.

To everyone who helped us by debating ideas, describing experiences, and sharing lessons learned—thank you. And a special thank you to the companies who agreed to let us tell their stories—your stories make the framework come to life and help motivate others to follow your lead. We trust this book adequately captures your insights and provides a useful tool for all enterprises on their journey to become future ready.

Stephanie's Personal Note

I'd like to start by thanking Peter and Ina. Peter and I have been research partners for over fifteen years, and brainstorming and working with Peter is exciting, intellectually rewarding, and best of all, fun! Peter has the uncanny ability to sniff out provocative ideas, often based on his latest workshops; he brings them back to our meetings so we can debate the concepts and experiment with new ways of measuring to push the research forward. I appreciate that he tests my thinking and encourages me to stretch. I would be remiss, however, if I let anyone think our partnership is all work. Peter and I share a love of cooking, and I never know when a photo of a new dish he is trying out is going to pop up in my text messages. Ina started working with us on a research project on partnering and ecosystems. She is a terrific case writer and is attuned to capturing the details and complexity of a case. It's been a joy working with Peter and Ina on this book.

My MIT CISR colleagues support and encourage me, critique my work, help me figure out where to take the research, and make my work better. Thank you all.

My family gives meaning to my life. My children, Max, Jack, and Zoe, and my daughter-in-law Chris, are all adults now, and it has been satisfying watching them make their ways into the world. I am so proud of them and delighted by who they are. My parents, Charles and Judith Woerner, have always given me unconditional love, and I couldn't wish for better parents. I am lucky to have John and Pris Chase as my in-laws. My mother-in-law passed away during the editing of this book, and I am privileged that my husband and I were able to spend time with her and support her during her last months. My siblings and I—Charlie, Susan, Mary, Teresa, and Ruth—became even closer during the pandemic. I'm glad we've made it a priority to talk to each other regularly in weekly family calls, and I love the family text chat— it's an ongoing exchange of important information, day-to-day details, and intermittent celebrations.

The Covid-19 pandemic has been lonely and isolating, and connecting with friends and family (thank you, Zoom) has helped immensely. Lot and Sheri Bates have been terrific neighbors—they've watched our kids and our pets over the years (and we theirs), they keep our extra house key, and they are always around when we need help or just want to chat for a bit. I've kept up lively conversations about work, children, craft, and cooking with Tina Underwood and Susie Hebert, and I am hoping to see them in person soon. My book group—Ariane Belkadi, Peggy Boning, Karen Estrella, and Sally Shelton—has been a monthly treat to look forward to. My yoga teacher, Carol Faulkner, who was not particularly comfortable with digital technologies, threw herself into learning how to conduct a class online, and I treasure the space she created and the support that all her students extend to each other. I am grateful for you all.

I'd also like to thank several professionals who have contributed greatly to my work and personal life. Dr. Eleanor Counselman has been a long-time listener and advisor, helping me understand myself better. Dr. Pamela Enders is my executive coach, encouraging me and offering advice as I tackle work challenges. I have recently started working with Jed Diamond, head of acting at the University of Tennessee, Knoxville, and I never knew my voice could do the things he has taught me to do.

I'll end with a big thank you to my husband, David Chase, for all his love, support, and encouragement. Raising a family and working full-time is a challenge, and David has been a partner through all of the struggles and joys. I have so much fun talking and sharing ideas with him. I'm looking forward to traveling and exploring and spending even more time together. Hugs and kisses, David!

Peter's Personal Note

As I celebrate my twenty-second anniversary at MIT and finish my tenth book, I reflect on the wonderful journey I've been on.

Acknowledgments

It's been a privilege and an exciting quest I have followed to try and understand the answer to one question: How do larger companies create more business value with technology and, more recently, how do they thrive in the era of digital ecosystems? What is fascinating about seeking to answer this question is that some aspects of success have not changed over all those years (e.g., the ability to embrace change), while others, including technology and how we partner, have changed radically in the digital era (e.g., business models, cloud-enabled services, and digital partnering).

The foundational stage in this wonderful journey began when I was a doctoral student in the IS department at the New York University Stern School of Business. I was privileged to work with some of the best people in the field and to have their support while I learned how to do research. A big thank you to Hank Lucas, Jon Turner, Margrethe Olson, Ted Stohr, Wanda Orlikowski, and Ken Laudon (deceased).

It's been a great pleasure to go on this journey with Stephanie and Ina. Stephanie and I have worked together for more than fifteen years. This is our second book together, and we have written many papers and MIT CISR research briefings. We complement each other's skills particularly well, and I always enjoy our many research meetings debating issues, analyzing data, extracting insights, and simplifying messages. Stephanie is the most talented data analyst I've ever worked with and can make even reluctant data tell their story. But it is perhaps Stephanie's ability to manage multiple projects and deal with the inevitable setbacks and challenges that research projects always encounter, with good cheer and only the occasional curse, that makes her so productive and such a great colleague.

For this book, we welcomed Ina to the team. Ina is a talented case researcher and has a great ability to crystallize key messages that help case studies tell stories rather than just relate facts.

Acknowledgments

A huge thank you to Dorothea Gray. As with the last one, Dorothea has made many contributions to this book, perhaps the most challenging of which was organizing me. In addition, Dorothea conducted research; set up interviews; created slides; produced transcripts; created presentation materials; put together countless workshops and talks; and worked with many of our member companies' boards, CEOs, and technology leaders. Dorothea makes it all look easy, despite juggling multiple priorities, conflicting deadlines, and impossible schedules. Thank you.

Over the twenty-two years I have been at MIT CISR, Chris Foglia has been my wonderful colleague, associate director, confidant, advisor, and completely reliable and insightful partner. Thank you, Chris, for everything you do for MIT CISR. Much of MIT CISR's success is your doing.

Thank you to six super-talented professionals without whom I couldn't have produced this book or done many other things. Thank you to Dr. Dean Eliott at Massachusetts Eye and Ear, who restored the sight in my left eye and has helped so many other patients. To Tim Schleiger, director and founder, and Alannah Miller, pilates teacher at the Sports Clinic of Melbourne, thank you for keeping me ready for the next gig. Many thanks to lifelong friend Jed Diamond, head of acting at the University of Tennessee, Knoxville, and Dr. Debbie Phyland at Voice Medicine Australia for making my voice work well despite talking too much; and to John Sarno at NYU (deceased) for pioneering a mind-body understanding and healing of back pain.

I would like to dedicate this book to Emily and Parker, the two newest members of the Australian Weill clan, and to Charlotte and Ava Leski. It is really for you and your generation that we work to understand how to make a better future. And to all the other members of my Aussie family: Steve, Lois, David, Marta, Simon, Amy, and Olivia—thank you for helping make it all worthwhile.

A warm welcome to the world for the Leski twins. I have a feeling that given your folks, Adam and Bec, you will be digital divas and lead us to the next level of digital savvy.

To my wife, Margi Olson, my true love and partner in life: big hugs and thank you. Thank you for finding a way to enjoy our crazy schedule traveling the globe and making it fun. Thank you for always wanting to understand what I was talking about, even when I was still forming the ideas. Thank you for encouraging me to pursue this journey of discovery and being my partner along the way. I look forward to many more walks together, discussing the next big question that fascinates us.

Ina's Personal Note

Thank you to my coauthors, Stephanie Woerner and Peter Weill, for the inspiring collaboration on this book and other MIT CISR research. I am also grateful to my MIT CISR colleagues and mentors, especially those mentioned in our common acknowledgments. My work has also benefited significantly from the guidance of other mentors and friends. I would like to specifically thank Elizabeth Davidson and Jody Hoffer Gittell for their support. I would like to thank my husband, Benjamin Okun; my mother, Ursula Sebastian; and my father, Dr. Hans-Jürgen Sebastian, for their love and support. To my father: how lucky I was to have you! I miss you more than words can say.

About the Authors

STEPHANIE L. WOERNER is director and a research scientist at the Center for Information Systems Research (CISR) at the MIT Sloan School of Management. MIT CISR has approximately eighty-five company members globally who use, debate, support, and participate in the research. Stephanie studies how companies use technology and data to create more effective business models and how they manage the associated organizational change. Her coauthored articles include "Thriving in an Increasingly Digital Ecosystem" (named one of the top articles of the decade by SMR), "It Pays to Have a Digitally Savvy Board," and "Does Your C-Suite Have Enough Digital Smarts?" in *Sloan Management Review*. In 2018, Stephanie and Peter Weill published *What's Your Digital Business Model? Six Questions to Help You Build the Next-Generation Enterprise* (Harvard Business Review Press, 2018).

Stephanie has done presentations and workshops for top management teams and boards of large global firms, been a subject matter expert for the *Wall Street Journal* CEO Council, and moderated a number of panels, including one on the future of financial services for the Federal Reserve. She earned her PhD in Organizational Behavior from the Stanford Graduate School of Business.

PETER WEILL is a passionate researcher, speaker, facilitator, and student of what companies need to do to succeed in the digital economy. He is the chairman emeritus and part-time senior research scientist at MIT Center for Information Systems Research (CISR) which studies and works with companies on how to transform for success in the digital era.

This is Peter's seventh coauthored Harvard Business Review Press book. He has also published in *MIT Sloan Management Review*, *Harvard Business Review*, the *Wall Street Journal*, and academic outlets. Ziff Davis recognized Weill as #24 of "The Top 100 Most Influential People in IT" and the highest-ranked academic. He has worked on digitization issues with the executive committees and boards of more than fifty companies globally.

Peter is enjoying a portfolio career including helping lead the MIT Sloan executive education programs for digitally savvy board members and top leadership teams plus being a strategic advisor to Insight Partners to identify best practices for leading transformations to Future Ready companies.

INA M. SEBASTIAN studies how large organizations transform for success in the digital economy. Her research focuses on partnering in digital ecosystems. She is particularly interested in how companies coordinate ecosystem collaboration when they partner across industries and sectors in fundamentally new ways to solve complex challenges.

Ina is a research scientist at the MIT Sloan Management School's Center for Information Systems Research (CISR). Before joining MIT CISR in 2014, she completed a PhD in International Management with a focus on Information Systems at the University of Hawaii, where she studied the role of digital technologies for coordination in multidisciplinary healthcare teams. Before her doctoral work, she was an industry analyst in the Bay Area.

Ina's publications on digital ecosystems, digital strategies and organizational redesign, and the digital workplace have appeared in *MIT Sloan Management Review*, *Management Information Systems Quarterly Executive*, and academic outlets.